# PUNK.

Loud Guitars, Louder Statements

This is for my Punk Crew back in our school days

&

The Emmanuel College Class of '99...

For putting up with our shit

# MANIFESTO

# Catalyst.

In the dimly lit back rooms of history, where societal upheaval, artistic rebellion, and audacious dissent converge, a cultural revolution was brewing. It was the late 1970s, a time when music was dominated by disco beats, progressive rock epics, and saccharine pop melodies. But from the gritty streets of New York City to the dingy pubs of London, a seismic shift was occurring, a cultural phenomenon that would come to be known as punk.

This movement was no mere trend; it was a catalyst for change—a roaring and unapologetic response to the status quo. It was an eruption of sound and fury that shattered convention, reshaped fashion, and challenged prevailing ideologies. Punk was the audacious refusal to accept the mundane, the embodiment of rebellion in its purest form. It was a vibrant, confrontational, and often controversial force that transcended its origins to become a global cultural phenomenon.

In this comprehensive exploration, we embark on a journey through the vibrant and tumultuous world of punk. "PUNK: Loud Guitars, Louder Statements" delves deep into the heart of a subculture that refuses to be silenced. This book is an ode to the rebels, the misfits, and the iconoclasts who forged a path through a world that desperately needed shaking up.

Picture this: a dimly lit, underground club in New York City. The air is thick with the acrid scent of cigarette smoke and the palpable anticipation of rebellion. On the stage, a band of young musicians, clad in tattered clothes and leather jackets, launches into a cacophony of raw, unapologetic sound. The audience, a diverse and eclectic mix of individuals, is united by a shared spirit of defiance. This is the world of punk, a world where loud guitars and even louder statements reign supreme.

At the heart of punk's allure is its unapologetic rejection of the mainstream. In the late 1970s, when disco's glossy beats and the sprawling compositions of progressive rock held sway over the music industry, punk emerged as a defiant counterpoint. It was a reaction to the excesses of the era, a call to strip away the pretentiousness and return to the raw, visceral core of rock 'n' roll.

The stereotypical punk, as seen in the clubs and on the streets of punk strongholds like New York and London, was a rebel with a cause, a living embodiment of the movement's ethos. Their appearance was a deliberate rejection of conventional fashion, an act of defiance against a world that sought to impose conformity.

A stereotypical punk might be visualized as follows: Their attire, often a collage of contradictions, featured torn and safety-pinned clothing that seemed more like a battle flag than a fashion statement. A leather jacket, adorned with patches and slogans, bore the battle scars of countless mosh pits. Ripped jeans, once functional but now more holes than denim, proudly displayed the wear and tear of rebellion. And then there were the combat boots—sturdy, well-worn, and emblematic of a subculture ready for a fight.

Tattoos and piercings adorned their bodies, each marking a personal statement of defiance and identity. Vibrant hair dyed in shades that ranged from electric blue to fiery red or jet black, often styled in unruly spikes or dramatic asymmetry, was a bold declaration of non-conformity. Facial expressions were serious, eyes lined with kohl, reflecting a mixture of intensity, anger, and determination.

But beyond the outward appearance, it was the attitude that truly defined the stereotypical punk. It was an attitude of resistance, a rejection of the norm, and a fierce commitment to authenticity. Punks were not content to simply exist within the boundaries of the status quo; they aimed to challenge, disrupt, and transform it. It was a rebellion against the notion that success and legitimacy required adherence to conventional standards of beauty or professionalism.

In this underground world, music was not a mere form of entertainment; it was a weapon of dissent. Punk lyrics were often confrontational, addressing themes of societal injustice, political corruption, and personal disillusionment. Bands like the Ramones, Sex Pistols, and The Clash channelled this discontent into blistering three-chord anthems that served as anthems for a generation searching for an outlet for their frustration.

But punk was not limited to music; it was a cultural movement that seeped into every aspect of life. It was a DIY ethos that championed self-expression and creativity. It was a rejection of consumerism in Favor of self-sufficiency. It was a call to action, a rallying cry for anyone who felt disillusioned by the world around them.

In "PUNK: Loud Guitars, Louder Statements," we dive deep into this world, exploring the roots, the music, the fashion, and the politics of punk. We trace its origins, meeting the pioneering icons who paved the way for a cultural revolution. We dissect the sonic revolution that was punk music, a revolution that discarded excess and embraced raw, unfiltered expression. We navigate the political undercurrents, the punk aesthetic, and the global reach of the movement. We examine its encounters with the mainstream, its evolution in the digital age, and its impact on gender norms. And we confront the controversies and challenges that have defined punk's journey.

Join us as we embark on a journey through the vibrant and tumultuous world of punk—a world where loud guitars and even louder statements have left an indelible mark on the cultural landscape. In the pages that follow, we'll dive headfirst into the chaos, the rebellion, and the unapologetic spirit of punk. This is a celebration of the misfits, the non-conformists, and the catalysts for change who continue to shape our world through the unstoppable force of punk.

# DIVISION.1

## Origins of Rebellion

In the darkened corridors of history, where the echoes of societal discord and artistic insurgency reverberate, a cultural revolution was stirring. The late 1970s marked an era dominated by disco's danceable beats, the sprawling epics of progressive rock, and the saccharine melodies of pop music. Yet, beneath this veneer of conformity, a seismic shift was underway, a transformative movement known as punk.

In this opening chapter, "Origins of Rebellion," we embark on a journey to uncover the foundational elements that laid the groundwork for punk's explosive emergence. It is a journey into the annals of rebellion, tracing the roots of punk back to the beatniks and countercultural movements of the mid-20th century. These precursors sowed the seeds of dissent, nurturing the spirit of non-conformity and individualism that would become the lifeblood of punk. As we delve into the rebellious literature and the tumultuous sociopolitical climate of the era, we will begin to understand the fervour, the passion, and the raw energy that ignited punk's audacious flame.

Our voyage into the origins of punk begins with the enigmatic Beat Generation, a group of writers who challenged the conventions of their time with radical literary expressions. Figures like Jack Kerouac, Allen Ginsberg, and William S. Burroughs were at the forefront of this literary rebellion, crafting works that rejected societal norms and championed individualism. Their prose and poetry brimmed with a sense of wanderlust, non-conformity, and a yearning for authenticity that would resonate with future generations of rebels.

The Beat Generation's rejection of the status quo and their embrace of unconventional lifestyles provided a template for countercultural movements to come. Their writings, often characterized by a raw and unfiltered voice, laid the intellectual groundwork for the defiant spirit that would later define punk.

Through this exploration, we gain insight into the Beatniks' influence on the cultural landscape, where rebellion thrived in the written word.

As we navigate further into the annals of rebellion, we arrive at the countercultural movements of the 1960s, a decade marked by fervent opposition to mainstream values and a yearning for social transformation. The rejection of traditional norms and the pursuit of alternative lifestyles became the calling cards of this era. In our examination of the broader countercultural movement, we discover the rejection of consumerism, the embrace of social activism, and the rise of anti-authoritarianism.

The youth of the 1960s, disillusioned with the prevailing establishment, took to the streets in protest. Iconic events like the Summer of Love and Woodstock bore witness to the power of music, unity, and social consciousness as forces for change. The counterculture was a breeding ground for non-conformist ideas and a crucible for dissent, setting the stage for a new era of rebellion. Through this exploration, we glean insights into the cultural shifts and aspirations that would become integral to punk's DNA.

As we conclude our journey through the "Origins of Rebellion," we turn our attention to the energetic and unrefined sounds of garage rock. Born in the 1960s, garage rock was the sonic embodiment of youthful rebellion, characterized by its raw, do-it-yourself ethos and unapologetic energy. Garage rock bands, often formed by young musicians with minimal resources, took the stage with a fervour and authenticity that resonated with audiences hungry for something real.

The influence of garage rock on punk was profound. These bands shattered conventions, embracing imperfection and unbridled passion over technical virtuosity. As we explore garage rock's raucous melodies and rebellious spirit, we begin to understand the music's role in nurturing dissent and providing a sonic canvas upon which punk's distinctive sound would be painted.

In the chapters that follow, we will delve deeper into the evolution of punk culture, tracing how these origins of rebellion culminated in the birth of punk as a powerful force for change and self-affirmation. We will explore how punk's rejection of traditional values and authority, coupled with its embrace of activism and dissent, would shape its music, fashion, and attitudes, creating a subculture that continues to inspire rebels and misfits to this day. Our journey through the origins of punk is only the beginning, as we move forward to witness the explosive emergence of a cultural phenomenon that refuses to be silenced.

# DIVISION.1-1

### Let's Start with a Beat

BACK IN THE '50S, YOU had this wild literary and culture scene spawn, the Beat Generation, suggests West, J. (2015). Let's dive deep into the vibes of the Beat Generation, see how they cranked up the counterculture scene, and planted the rebellious seeds that birthed the Punk revolution! Here, we will delve deep into the world of the Beatniks and the literary rebellion they ignited, which would ultimately become a cornerstone for the punk movement.

Palumbo, M. (2018) indicates the Beat Generation, a term coined by writer Jack Kerouac, was a collective of artists, poets, and thinkers who rejected the stifling conformity of post-war America in Favor of a radical, free-spirited existence. This group of non-conformists sought to break away from the constraints of mainstream culture and the materialism that had come to define American society in the 1950s. At the core of the Beat ethos was the celebration of individualism and a passionate rejection of societal norms. Beatniks believed in living authentically, embracing the raw experiences of life, and challenging the status quo. They were cultural rebels who paved the way for future generations of iconoclasts, including the punks of the late 1970s.

Within the Beat Generation, several key figures emerged as torchbearers of this literary and cultural rebellion. Palumbo, M. (2018) points out three luminaries in particular—Jack Kerouac, Allen Ginsberg, and William S. Burroughs—left an indelible mark on both Beat literature and the broader countercultural landscape.

Jack Kerouac, perhaps the most iconic figure of the Beat Generation, Kerouac is best known for his novel "On the Road." The novel was an ode to wanderlust, capturing the essence of the open road and the pursuit of personal freedom. Kerouac's spontaneous prose style mirrored the raw, unfiltered expression that would later characterize punk lyrics. His novel was a blueprint for the rejection of conventional lifestyles and a call to embrace the unconventional.

Allen Ginsberg's poem "Howl" is considered a masterpiece of Beat literature and a clarion call for non-conformity. In "Howl," Ginsberg denounced the conformity, materialism, and repression of the 1950s. His vivid, often controversial language celebrated individuality and unabashedly confronted societal ills. "Howl" was more than poetry; it was a battle cry for those who sought to break free from the shackles of convention.

William S. Burroughs, a writer known for his experimental and often surreal prose, explored themes of addiction, control, and authority in works like "Naked Lunch." His writing was a direct challenge to the establishment and a reflection of the subversive undercurrents that would become central to punk ideology. Burroughs' cutting-edge style and unapologetic critique of authority made him an inspiration to future generations of rebels.

The literary works of the Beat Generation were not just reflections of their time; they were manifestos of rebellion. The themes of non-conformity, individualism, and rebellion permeated Beat literature, providing a philosophical framework that would later find resonance in punk. Non-conformity was a recurring motif in Beat writings, epitomized by the rejection of societal norms and the celebration of the outsider. The Beats embraced a bohemian lifestyle that championed authenticity over conformity, living life on one's terms rather than succumbing to societal expectations.

Individualism was another pillar of Beat literature. Kerouac's "On the Road" exalted the individual's quest for self-discovery and adventure. Ginsberg's "Howl" celebrated the unique experiences and voices of those who dared to be different. Burroughs' exploration of personal freedom and the subconscious mind underscored the importance of individual expression.

Rebellion, in its many forms, was at the heart of Beat writings. Ginsberg's "Howl" rebelled against the stifling conformity of the 1950s, while Burroughs' "Naked Lunch" rebelled against the conventions of narrative structure and morality. Kerouac's exploration of the road was a rebellion against the constraints of settled life. These works were not just literary exercises; they were revolutionary declarations.

The 1960s marked a period of intense cultural and political ferment in the United States and around the world. This was an era when the younger generation began to question and reject the traditional values and norms of their parents and society at large. It was a time of rebellion against the established order—a rejection of the conformist, consumer-driven values that had dominated the post-war era. The countercultural movement of the 1960s was, at its core, a rejection of mainstream values. Young people, disillusioned by the materialism and conformity of the 1950s, sought to forge a new path. They challenged the prevailing norms regarding everything from gender roles to civil rights, from environmental consciousness to sexual liberation.

Central to the countercultural movement was a commitment to social activism and a fierce anti-authoritarianism. The youth of the 1960s were deeply engaged in political and social causes, advocating for civil rights, protesting the Vietnam War, and championing environmental and feminist movements. These activists rejected the notion that authority figures and institutions held all the answers, advocating for a more participatory and inclusive society. It was a time when the idea of "questioning authority" became a mantra for a generation. The counterculture celebrated DIY ethos, self-empowerment, and grassroots organizing. Communities formed around shared ideals and activism, often in opposition to the perceived excesses of the establishment. Two iconic events that encapsulated the spirit of the countercultural movement were the "Summer of Love" in 1967 and the Woodstock Festival in 1969.

In 1967, San Francisco's Haight-Ashbury district became ground zero for a cultural phenomenon known as the "Summer of Love." Thousands of young people flocked to the neighbourhood, drawn by the promise of a new way of life characterized by peace, love, and unity. It was a vibrant celebration of countercultural ideals, marked by music, art, and a rejection of materialism. The hippie movement, with its emphasis on communal living and non-violence, was a potent symbol of the rejection of mainstream values.

In August 1969, the Woodstock Festival, held in upstate New York, brought together over 400,000 people for a weekend of music and peace. Woodstock became a symbol of the counterculture's ability to organize large-scale, anti-authoritarian events that celebrated music, art, and social change. The festival featured iconic performances by artists like Jimi Hendrix, Janis Joplin, and The Who, and it reinforced the idea that music could be a powerful force for social and cultural transformation.

These events, among many others, stand as powerful testaments to the countercultural movement's remarkable capacity to challenge entrenched norms and reshape the fabric of society. In the tumultuous landscape of the 1960s, they served as luminous beacons of hope and transformation, embodying the spirit of rebellion against the established order. By gathering together thousands of like-minded individuals, these events demonstrated the profound influence of music, art, and communal solidarity in fomenting social change and undermining the hold of mainstream values. They showcased how these countercultural gatherings could serve as crucibles for the forging of a new cultural and social identity—one that prized individuality, peace, and unity over conformity and division. These moments in time, where utopian ideals and artistic expression converged, would reverberate in the hearts of the punks who would follow, inspiring their own audacious quest for rebellion and change.

# DIVISION.1-2

### The Counterculture Movement

TO UNDERSTAND THE EMERGENCE and evolution of punk culture in the late 1970s, we must first delve into the socio-political climate of the era. The 1970s was a decade marked by upheaval, conflict, and transformation, with a backdrop of significant events that profoundly influenced the music, attitudes, and values of the time.

One of the defining and most contentious issues of the 1970s was the Vietnam War. This conflict, which had its roots in the 1950s, continued to cast a long shadow over American society throughout the decade. The war had sparked widespread opposition and protests by the late 1960s, with young people at the forefront of the anti-war movement. As the 1970s dawned, the war's toll was evident. The American public had grown increasingly disillusioned with the government's handling of the conflict and the human cost of the war. The draft, which conscripted young men to serve in the military, was a source of anger and resentment among the youth. The anti-war movement, often led by college students, brought millions to the streets in protest.

The Vietnam War had a profound impact on the counterculture and the music of the era. Tunes such as Edwin Starr's "War" and Creedence Clearwater Revival's "Fortunate Son" morphed into rallying cries for anti-establishment emotions, capturing the youthful anger and discontent. Punk, with its rebellious ethos and confrontational stance, would draw from the anti-war movement's spirit of dissent.

The 1970s also witnessed the ongoing struggle for civil rights in the United States. While the Civil Rights Act of 1964 had been a landmark achievement in the fight against racial discrimination, racial tensions persisted. The decade saw the emergence of new challenges, including efforts to address economic disparities and systemic racism.

The Black Power movement, which had gained momentum in the late 1960s, continued to advocate for self-determination and equality for Black Americans. Icons like Angela Davis and Huey Newton were prominent figures in the movement, advocating for radical change. The fight for racial equality remained a potent force, and punk, as a subculture, would grapple with issues of race and social justice.

Perhaps no event captured the disillusionment and erosion of trust in American institutions more than the Watergate scandal. The early 1970s were marred by revelations of political misconduct and corruption at the highest levels of government. The break-in at the Democratic National Committee headquarters in the Watergate complex and subsequent cover-up by the Nixon administration shook the foundations of American democracy.

The scandal, which unfolded over several years and culminated in President Richard Nixon's resignation in 1974, left an indelible mark on the American psyche. It eroded faith in political leaders and institutions, fostering a sense of cynicism and scepticism among the population. Punk, with its rejection of authority and emphasis on individualism, would echo this sentiment of distrust in the establishment.

The 1970s was also marked by economic uncertainty and an energy crisis. The OPEC oil embargo of 1973 led to soaring gasoline prices and long lines at gas stations, highlighting America's vulnerability to foreign oil dependence. High inflation and unemployment rates added to the economic instability.

These challenges impacted the daily lives of Americans, influencing their attitudes and priorities. The economic uncertainties of the era would find expression in punk music, which often addressed issues of alienation, economic hardship, and the pursuit of authenticity in a world marked by uncertainty. The 1970s was a turbulent decade, characterized by a perfect storm of socio-political upheaval, disillusionment, and cultural change. The Vietnam War, civil rights movement, Watergate scandal, and economic challenges all contributed to a climate of discontent and distrust in established institutions. These events would serve as the backdrop against which punk culture would emerge and flourish.

As the 1970s unfolded, the youth of America found themselves at a crossroads. The countercultural movements of the 1960s had left an indelible mark on their collective consciousness. However, many young people were eager to forge their own path, seeking alternative means of rebellion that departed from the ideals and tactics of their predecessors.

Punk culture would emerge as a response to this quest for new forms of rebellion. It rejected the idealism and optimism of the 1960s, embracing a gritty, confrontational attitude. Punk was a revolt against the commodification of rebellion and a rejection of the notion that social change could be achieved through peace and love alone. It represented a break from the past while preserving the spirit of defiance that had defined the youth movements of the previous decade.

One of the defining characteristics of youth rebellion in the 1970s was a wholesale rejection of traditional values and authority structures. The youth were disillusioned with the institutions that had guided previous generations. Conformity, consumerism, and the pursuit of the "American Dream" were viewed with scepticism. Punk culture, with its DIY ethos and anti-establishment stance, epitomized this rejection of traditional values and authority. Punk fashion, characterized by torn clothing, wild hairstyles, and unconventional accessories, challenged conventional notions of appearance and beauty. Punk music, with its raw, unpolished sound and confrontational lyrics, defied the mainstream music industry's standards of professionalism and marketability.

The 1970s was a fertile ground for activism and protests across a spectrum of issues. Young people were at the forefront of movements advocating for social justice, equality, and environmental awareness. The civil rights movement, although it had made significant strides in the 1960s, continued to inspire activism in the pursuit of racial equality. Additionally, the feminist movement gained momentum, challenging traditional gender roles and advocating for women's rights. Environmentalism saw the emergence of organizations like Greenpeace, dedicated to addressing ecological concerns. These movements were characterized by their youthful energy and idealism, with young activists playing central roles in effecting change.

Punk culture, too, would embrace a spirit of activism and protest. Punk bands often used their music as a platform to address social and political issues, from nuclear disarmament to police brutality. Punk shows became spaces where like-minded individuals could come together to express their discontent and rally for change. The ethos of rebellion and activism converged in punk, as the subculture encouraged its followers to question the status quo and challenge authority.

The 1970s also witnessed the emergence of various cultural movements and subcultures that celebrated nonconformity and individuality. These movements offered young people alternative identities and spaces for self-expression. For example, the disco subculture embraced hedonism and escapism, providing a counterpoint to the prevailing seriousness of the era. Punk, in contrast, rejected the shallowness of disco and sought to expose the darker realities of society. The punk subculture, with its emphasis on authenticity and rebellion, provided a sense of belonging to those who felt alienated from mainstream culture.

Similarly, the skateboarding subculture emerged in the 1970s, offering young people an outlet for physical expression and a sense of belonging. Skateboarding was an inherently countercultural activity, as it often took place in urban landscapes where skaters reclaimed public spaces for their own use. Punk music and skateboarding shared an affinity for outsider status and a rejection of conventional norms.

The youth of the 1970s were characterized by a thirst for authenticity and rebellion. They sought to carve out their own identities, rejecting the values and authority structures that had shaped previous generations. The era was marked by a vibrant tapestry of activism, protests, and cultural movements that provided young people with outlets for dissent and self-expression.

Punk culture, emerging from this cauldron of discontent and rebellion, would become a symbol of this quest for authenticity and defiance. It encapsulated the spirit of a generation that had grown weary of empty promises and conformity. Punk's confrontational attitude, DIY ethos, and emphasis on individuality would resonate deeply with those seeking a genuine, unfiltered form of expression in a world marked by disillusionment and unrest.

# DIVISION.1-3

**Garage Days**

Another chapter in the annals of music history in the 1960s, is the story of profound transformation and innovation, marked by the emergence of a raucous and rebellious genre known as garage rock. This underground movement, characterized by its raw, DIY sound and a ferocious spirit of independence, would play a pivotal role in shaping the sonic landscape that would eventually give birth to punk.

To understand the rise of garage rock, we must first peel back the layers of the 1960s music scene. It was a time when mainstream music was dominated by the polished sounds of Motown, the British Invasion, and folk-rock. But beneath the glossy surface, a raw and unrefined counter-movement was brewing in the garages and basements of suburban America. This was garage rock—an antithesis to the sophisticated studio productions of the era.

Garage rock was, at its core, a grassroots rebellion against the commercialization of music. Young, often self-taught musicians, inspired by the simplicity of rock 'n' roll pioneers like Chuck Berry and Little Richard, picked up their instruments and embraced the DIY ethos. They recorded their music on rudimentary equipment, often with minimal technical expertise, giving birth to a sound that was undeniably authentic and unpolished. Central to the garage rock movement were bands that exemplified the gritty, lo-fi sound that would become its hallmark. These bands, often formed by high school friends or neighbourhood acquaintances, shared a passion for making music that was loud, raucous, and immediate.

What set garage rock apart was its unapologetic rebellion and unbridled energy. These bands weren't concerned with virtuosic musicianship or polished production; they were focused on making music that was immediate and authentic. This rawness, coupled with a fierce determination to be heard, was the heartbeat of garage rock. Garage rock lyrics often spoke to the frustrations and longings of youth, touching on themes of love, alienation, and the desire to break free from societal constraints. The simplicity of the music allowed for a direct and visceral connection with listeners. It was music that didn't ask for permission; it demanded attention.

The rebellious spirit of garage rock extended beyond the music itself. Bands often performed in unconventional venues, from basements and garages to local clubs and high school dances. These grassroots performances were characterized by a contagious energy, with bands and audiences feeding off each other's enthusiasm. It was a scene that thrived on the DIY ethos, where anyone with a guitar and a passion for rebellion could become a part of the movement.

In this crucible of creativity and rebellion, garage rock bands honed their craft, experimenting with distortion, feedback, and unconventional song structures. They rejected the notion that music had to be polished and refined, opting instead for a visceral and immediate approach. This rejection of conformity and embrace of imperfection would become a defining trait of punk.

The raw energy and rebellious spirit of garage rock would find its echo in the punk ethos. It was a spirit that refused to be tamed, a sound that was unapologetically loud and uncompromising—a sound that would lay the foundation for a musical revolution yet to come... Proto-punk, a musical movement that incubated the punk ethos and helped shape the course of musical rebellion. We'll introduce some of the influential bands and artists who played a pivotal role in this transitional period, such as The Stooges, MC5, and The Velvet Underground. These pioneers of proto-punk were united by their experimental sound, provocative lyrics, and an unwavering rejection of mainstream norms.

One of the most iconic bands to emerge from the proto-punk landscape was The Stooges, hailing from Ann Arbor, Michigan. Led by the enigmatic and volatile Iggy Pop, The Stooges embodied the raw, unapologetic spirit that would come to define punk. Their self-titled debut album, released in 1969, was a sonic explosion of primal energy. Songs like "1969" and "I Wanna Be Your Dog" were charged with Iggy's frenetic stage presence and provocative lyrics, challenging societal conventions and pushing boundaries.

The Stooges' music was characterized by a stripped-down, garage rock-inspired sound that fused with a sense of nihilism and rebellion. Their onstage antics, marked by Iggy Pop's self-destructive behaviour and interaction with the audience, left an indelible mark on the punk aesthetic. The Stooges were fearless pioneers, unafraid to confront the darkest corners of human experience and give voice to the disaffected youth.

Another Detroit-based band that blazed a trail toward punk was the MC5 (Motor City Five). Their incendiary debut album, "Kick Out the Jams" (1969), was a rallying cry for the counterculture. With tracks like the titular "Kick Out the Jams," the MC5 delivered a sonic manifesto of rebellion and anti-establishment fervour. The album's raw, live recording captured the band's blistering energy and unapologetic attitude.

MC5's music was heavily influenced by rock 'n' roll and R&B, yet it was the band's political consciousness and willingness to confront authority that set them apart. Songs like "Ramblin' Rose" and "Motor City Is Burning" addressed issues of social injustice and political unrest, reflecting the turbulent times in which they lived. The MC5's fearless advocacy for change and their electrifying performances laid a foundation for the punk movement's confrontational approach.

In the heart of New York City's burgeoning artistic scene, The Velvet Underground, led by Lou Reed and John Cale, were crafting a unique sound that defied categorization. While not as explicitly aggressive as some of their proto-punk counterparts, their experimental approach to music and lyrics made them trailblazers of punk's avant-garde edge. Their 1967 debut album, "The Velvet Underground & Nico," remains a landmark in rock history.

The Velvet Underground's music was marked by its dissonance, experimentation, and unfiltered portrayal of taboo subjects such as drug addiction, sadomasochism, and urban decay. Songs like "Heroin" and "Venus in Furs" explored the darker corners of human existence, challenging societal norms and pushing artistic boundaries. Their connection to the counterculture and the burgeoning punk scene of New York City positioned them as artistic provocateurs whose influence would be felt far beyond their contemporaries.

What united these proto-punk pioneers was their shared commitment to challenging the status quo in music and society. They embraced an experimental sound that defied conventions, often incorporating dissonant guitar work, unconventional song structures, and a rejection of polished production. Their lyrics were provocative and unapologetic, addressing themes of rebellion, nihilism, social unrest, and personal alienation.

Proto-punk artists rejected mainstream norms, opting for a confrontational approach that mirrored the disillusionment and anger of the era. They did not seek commercial success or acceptance; instead, they were dedicated to pushing boundaries, provoking thought, and rejecting the trappings of a conformist society. These artists were the bridge between garage rock's grassroots rebellion and punk's explosive emergence, paving the way for the punk movement to flourish in the years to come.

In the grand tapestry of music history, certain albums emerge as catalysts, reshaping genres, and revitalizing forgotten sounds. "Nuggets: Original Artyfacts from the First Psychedelic Era, 1965–1968" is one such album. Released in 1972, this compilation served as a time capsule, unearthing a treasure trove of obscure garage rock gems from the 1960s. It played a pivotal role in rekindling interest in garage rock, propelling these long-forgotten songs into the limelight and leaving an indelible mark on the trajectory of punk music.

The 1960s were a fertile breeding ground for rock 'n' roll, producing countless bands that took to garages, basements, and makeshift studios to craft their own brand of rebellious music. Many of these bands operated in relative obscurity, producing singles that rarely received airplay beyond their local scenes. By the early 1970s, the garage rock sound was a distant memory, overshadowed by the polished productions of the era.

Enter Lenny Kaye, a musician and writer with a deep appreciation for rock's rebellious roots. Kaye was tapped by Elektra Records to compile an album that would unearth these forgotten garage rock treasures. The result was "Nuggets," a 27-track collection that showcased the raw energy, simplicity, and infectious hooks of these long-lost songs. "Nuggets" achieved the remarkable feat of resurrecting obscure garage rock songs and introducing them to a new generation of music enthusiasts. The album was a revelation, unearthing hidden gems that had languished in obscurity for years. Songs like The Electric Prunes' "I Had Too Much to Dream (Last Night)," The Seeds' "Pushin' Too Hard," and The Standells' "Dirty Water" burst forth with an energy and authenticity that resonated with listeners.

What made "Nuggets" particularly potent was its ability to capture the zeitgeist of the 1960s. These songs, often recorded on shoestring budgets, exuded a rebellious spirit that mirrored the counterculture of the era. They were anthems of youthful defiance, addressing themes of love, rebellion, and alienation with an unpolished honesty. In many ways, these songs were a sonic representation of the rebellious spirit that would later find its home in punk. The impact of "Nuggets" extended far beyond its role as a revivalist compilation. It became a foundational influence on the burgeoning punk rock movement of the mid-1970s. As punk musicians sought to distance themselves from the excesses of mainstream rock and return to the genre's raw, unfiltered roots, "Nuggets" provided a blueprint.

Punk musicians found inspiration in the unpretentious, DIY ethos of the garage rock bands featured on the album. The songs on "Nuggets" celebrated imperfection and authenticity over technical prowess. Punk embraced this philosophy, rejecting the notion that virtuosity was a prerequisite for making meaningful music. Bands like The Ramones, The Sex Pistols, and The Clash, who would go on to define punk, drew from the rebellious, stripped-down spirit of "Nuggets."

Moreover, "Nuggets" introduced punk musicians to the idea that music could be a vehicle for personal expression and rebellion. The garage rock songs on the album were not concerned with commercial success or conformity; they were visceral expressions of the bands' identities and frustrations. This ethos resonated deeply with the punk movement, which sought to break free from the constraints of the music industry and mainstream society.

"Nuggets" left an enduring legacy that continues to influence musicians to this day. It sparked a renewed interest in garage rock, leading to the rediscovery of countless obscure bands and songs. Moreover, it served as a bridge between the garage rock of the 1960s and the punk explosion of the late 1970s, providing punk musicians with a blueprint for their own rebellious sound and attitude. Beyond its musical influence, "Nuggets" was a cultural touchstone that celebrated the uncompromising spirit of rock 'n' roll. It reminded listeners that music could be a vehicle for rebellion, a means of expressing dissatisfaction with the status quo, and a channel for embracing authenticity and individuality.

# LAST.TRACK.

IN THIS SECTION, WE have embarked on a journey through the cultural, musical, and historical elements that laid the groundwork for the emergence of punk culture in the late 1970s. We have explored the Beat Generation and countercultural roots, the turbulent socio-political climate of the 1970s, and the youth rebellion and dissent that characterized the era. These elements, while distinct, converged to form a potent crucible of influences that would give birth to punk as we know it.

The Beat Generation, with its themes of non-conformity and individualism, laid the intellectual foundations for countercultural movements that rejected mainstream values and sought alternative forms of expression. The 1970s, marked by disillusionment with government, social unrest, and the rejection of traditional values, created an atmosphere ripe for rebellion and cultural transformation. The youth of the era, searching for new avenues of dissent, embraced activism, protests, and cultural movements that celebrated nonconformity and individuality.

As we move forward in our exploration of punk culture, we will witness the evolution of these influences into the punk movement of the late 1970s. The cultural and historical elements we have examined will converge with the musical and artistic expressions of punk, creating a subculture that defied convention, embraced DIY ethos, and channelled the frustrations and aspirations of a generation. Punk, as a cultural phenomenon, was not merely a response to its predecessors; it was a revolution in its own right, a roaring and unapologetic catalyst for change that transcended its origins to become a global force of rebellion and authenticity.

In the upcoming sections, we will trace the journey of punk from its roots to its explosive emergence on the music scene. We will delve into the music, fashion, attitudes, and politics that define punk, exploring how it harnessed the spirit of rebellion, dissent, and authenticity we have uncovered here. Join us as we dive into the heart of punk culture, where loud guitars and even louder statements would forever alter the cultural landscape.

# DIVISION.2

## Renegades of Punk

In the annals of music history, certain chapters stand as monuments to rebellion and revolution, reshaping the sonic landscape and challenging the very essence of the mainstream. As we journey through the enthralling world of punk culture, we arrive at a chapter adorned with leather jackets, snarls of defiance, and the raw energy of a musical revolution. This is the chapter of "Renegades of Punk," where we delve deep into the lives and legacies of three bands that became synonymous with the punk movement: The Ramones, The Sex Pistols, and The Clash.

These bands, whose names still resonate with fans and music enthusiasts alike, were the vanguards of a genre that rejected the gloss and glamour of the music industry in Favor of unapologetic authenticity. In this chapter, we explore how The Ramones, The Sex Pistols, and The Clash ignited a cultural wildfire, inspiring countless others to pick up instruments, raise their voices, and defy convention.

Our journey commences with the relentless energy and the trademark uniformity of The Ramones. Hailing from the streets of Queens, New York City, this band of misfits turned rock 'n' roll on its head. With their signature leather jackets, torn jeans, and unruly hair, The Ramones were the embodiment of punk's do-it-yourself ethos. But it was their music that truly shook the foundations of the industry.

The Ramones' sound was characterized by its simplicity and speed, stripped of excess and polished production. Their songs, often brief but endlessly catchy, became anthems of rebellion. With tracks like "Blitzkrieg Bop" and "I Wanna Be Sedated," they captured the frustrations and yearnings of disenchanted youth. The Ramones provided an antidote to the pretentiousness of the era's music, delivering punk's message with three-chord fury and infectious hooks.

Our exploration of punk's pioneers takes us to the tumultuous streets of London, where The Sex Pistols emerged as the embodiment of punk's confrontational spirit. Led by the enigmatic and controversial figurehead, Johnny Rotten, The Sex Pistols were agents of chaos in a conservative society. Their music, epitomized by tracks like "Anarchy in the U.K." and "God Save the Queen," was a blistering assault on the establishment.

The Sex Pistols challenged authority with their confrontational lyrics and anarchic performances, inciting outrage and fascination in equal measure. Their notorious breakup during the Jubilee Year of 1977 only added to their mystique, cementing their status as punk icons. The Sex Pistols gave voice to the disenfranchised, embodying the frustration and alienation of a generation.

As we traverse the punk landscape, we encounter The Clash, a band that combined the fiery energy of punk with a socially conscious edge. Their music was a potent cocktail of rebellion and activism, addressing issues like racism, social injustice, and political apathy. Tracks such as "London Calling" and "Should I Stay or Should I Go" became anthems that transcended the boundaries of punk.

The Clash's willingness to tackle pressing societal problems distinguished them from many of their peers. Their lyrics were a call to arms, encouraging listeners to question authority and embrace their inner renegade. With their diverse musical influences and politically charged message, The Clash demonstrated that punk could be a vehicle for change as well as a celebration of rebellion.

In the chapters that follow, we will delve deeper into the lives, music, and cultural impact of these trailblazing bands. We will trace their journeys from the fringes of the music scene to the forefront of a cultural revolution. Through their stories, we will explore how The Ramones, The Sex Pistols, and The Clash became the standard-bearers of punk, forever leaving their mark on the world of music and rebellion. Join us as we unearth the untamed spirits of these "Renegades of Punk" and the indelible legacies they forged.

# DIVISION.2-1

## Blitzkrieg Boppers

IN THE TUMULTUOUS LANDSCAPE of punk's inception, where rebellion was the anthem and authenticity the ultimate currency, few bands left an indelible mark quite like The Ramones. As we embark on this chapter, we venture into the heart of punk's birthplace: New York City. Here, in the grit and grime of the Lower East Side, a band of misfits and visionaries came together to ignite a musical revolution that would echo through the ages.

The Ramones, with their leather jackets, torn jeans, and dishevelled hair, were not merely musicians; they were the embodiment of punk's defiant ethos. With their raw energy and stripped-down sound, they carved a path that challenged the very essence of rock 'n' roll. In this chapter, we delve into the lives, music, and cultural significance of The Ramones, tracing their journey from obscurity to legendary status.

In the pages that follow, we will journey through the life, music, and legacy of The Ramones. We will uncover the rebellious spirit that defined this band and learn how their pursuit of authenticity and their disdain for the mainstream reshaped the course of rock 'n' roll history. Join us as we explore the pioneering spirit of The Ramones and celebrate the legacy of a band that continues to inspire rebels and misfits across the globe.

## The 6'6" Godfather of Punk Rock

Born Jeffrey Hyman on May 19, 1951, in Queens, New York, Joey Ramone would become the iconic frontman of The Ramones. His early life was marked by both challenges and a deep love for music. Growing up in the Forest Hills neighbourhood of Queens, Joey's childhood was not without difficulties. Brenner, B (2016) points out Joey Ramone battled both a severe case of obsessive-compulsive disorder (OCD) and the alienation that often accompanies being different. Despite these challenges, music became his refuge and a means of self-expression.

Joey's passion for music was evident from a young age. He gravitated towards rock 'n' roll, immersing himself in the sounds of artists like The Beatles and The Who. Inspired by their music, he started playing the drums and later took on the role of lead singer. His distinctive, gravelly voice would go on to become one of the defining features of The Ramones' sound.

Before adopting the name "Joey Ramone," he briefly performed under the moniker "Jeff Starship" as part of a glam rock band called Sniper. Gilmore, M. (2016) suggests it was in 1974 that Joey Ramone and his childhood friends—Johnny, Dee Dee, and Tommy Ramone—formed The Ramones. The Ramones' unique style and Joey's distinctive vocals quickly set them apart from the musical landscape of the time. With his lanky frame, signature sunglasses, and omnipresent leather jacket, Joey Ramone became an iconic figure in punk rock, an inspiration to countless aspiring musicians and a beacon of individuality.

### A Future Guitar Legend

John Cummings, known to the world as Johnny Ramone, was born on October 8, 1948, in Long Island, New York. Unlike Joey, Johnny's early life was marked by a relative stability. He grew up in a middle-class household in the suburban community of East Elmhurst, Queens. His love for music was ignited during his formative years when he saw the Beatles perform on the Ed Sullivan Show in 1964. This seminal moment sparked a passion for the guitar, and Johnny's life was forever changed.

Johnny's determination and discipline were evident from an early age. He dedicated himself to mastering the guitar, practicing relentlessly to achieve technical proficiency. His early influences included the likes of Jimi Hendrix and The Who's Pete Townshend, whose powerful and aggressive guitar playing would later influence The Ramones' sound.

Before co-founding The Ramones, Johnny played in a local band called Tangerine Puppets. However, it was in 1974, alongside Joey, Dee Dee, and Tommy Ramone, that he formed the band that would make him a punk rock legend. Johnny's minimalist, buzzsaw guitar style would become a defining element of The Ramones' sound, characterized by rapid power chords and a driving rhythm. His no-frills approach to guitar playing was a perfect complement to the band's stripped-down ethos.

Despite his often-gruff exterior, Johnny was known to be fiercely dedicated to the band and its success. He played an instrumental role in steering The Ramones to the pinnacle of punk rock prominence. His unrelenting commitment to punk purity and the band's unique vision solidified his legacy as one of punk's most influential guitarists.

**The Songwriter**

Born Douglas Colvin on September 18, 1951, in Fort Lee, Virginia, Dee Dee Ramone was the primary songwriter and bassist of The Ramones. His early life was marked by a sense of transience, as his family moved frequently due to his father's military career. This nomadic lifestyle exposed Dee Dee to a diverse array of cultures and musical influences, which would later find expression in his songwriting.

The family eventually settled in Forest Hills, Queens, where Dee Dee attended Forest Hills High School. It was during this period that he met Joey Ramone, forming a lifelong friendship that would serve as the foundation for The Ramones. Dee Dee's passion for music was undeniable, and he dabbled in various instruments before settling on the bass guitar.

Dee Dee's role as the primary songwriter of The Ramones was instrumental in shaping the band's distinctive sound. His lyrics often reflected the band's rebellious spirit, exploring themes of youth alienation, suburban ennui, and the trials of everyday life. Songs like "Now I Wanna Sniff Some Glue" and "Teenage Lobotomy" captured the essence of punk's defiance and youthful rebellion.

Despite his creative contributions, Dee Dee struggled with personal demons, including addiction issues. His battles with substance abuse would be a recurring theme throughout his life and career. Nonetheless, his songwriting prowess and musical innovation left an indelible mark on punk rock, and his legacy as a founding member of The Ramones remains undisputed.

Born Erdélyi Tamás on January 29, 1949, in Budapest, Hungary, Tommy Ramone was the original drummer and a vital architect of The Ramones' sound. His early life was shaped by a complex blend of cultural influences and the tumultuous backdrop of post-war Europe.

Tommy's family immigrated to the United States when he was a child, eventually settling in Forest Hills, Queens. As a young musician, Tommy developed a deep appreciation for folk music and bluegrass. This love for acoustic music would later influence his drumming style and songwriting within The Ramones.

Before becoming The Ramones' drummer, Tommy worked as an engineer and record producer. It was in this capacity that he would play a crucial role in shaping the band's debut album, "Ramones" (1976). Tommy's production work captured the band's raw energy and minimalist approach, helping to create the iconic sound that would define punk rock.

Tommy's drumming was characterized by its precision and minimalism, serving as the rhythmic backbone of The Ramones' music. His contributions to the band's early albums and his role as the original drummer established a foundation upon which The Ramones would build their legacy.

**The Ramones**

In the mid-1970s, the music scene was ripe for a revolution. The airwaves were saturated with sprawling prog-rock epics, polished disco beats, and sugary pop melodies. Glam rock had its glittering moment, and arena rock reigned supreme. Amidst this cacophony of convention, a band was born in the heart of New York City, one that would change the course of rock 'n' roll history forever. The Ramones, clad in leather jackets, torn jeans, and an attitude of unapologetic defiance, would emerge as the vanguards of a sonic revolution.

The late 1970s marked a period of upheaval and disillusionment, especially for the youth. The counterculture of the 1960s had given way to a sense of betrayal, with the Vietnam War dragging on, the civil rights movement facing continued struggles, and the Watergate scandal eroding trust in authority. It was a time of mounting frustration, and many young people were searching for a musical voice that resonated with their sense of alienation.

New York City, a hotbed of cultural diversity and creative energy, served as a fertile ground for musical experimentation. The city's clubs and dive bars became the breeding grounds for a burgeoning punk rock scene. Bands like The New York Dolls and Television were pushing the boundaries of music, embracing a raw, unpolished sound that rejected the pretentiousness of the era's rock.

It was against this backdrop of discontent and creative ferment that The Ramones emerged. Formed in 1974, the band's inception was not a calculated endeavour but a serendipitous convergence of like-minded misfits. Johnny, Joey, Dee Dee, and Tommy Ramone, four restless souls from the boroughs of Queens, came together with a shared vision: to strip away the excess, to reject the prevailing norms, and to create music that was a defiant cry against the mundane.

The Ramones' formation was not marked by extravagant auditions or grandiose plans. It was a simple, organic process. Johnny Ramone, the band's guitarist, initially encouraged the idea of forming a band with Joey Ramone, who had transitioned from playing the drums to taking on the role of lead singer. Dee Dee Ramone, the bassist and primary songwriter, rounded out the core trio. With their stripped-down, minimalist sound, they began to rehearse in a dank loft on Manhattan's East 2nd Street.

Early performances at venues like CBGB and Max's Kansas City were raw and visceral, marked by brevity and intensity. The Ramones' live shows were a revelation, with songs lasting just a few minutes, delivered in rapid succession, and punctuated by Joey's distinctive, gravelly vocals. It was a departure from the pomp and grandeur of contemporary rock acts, and it resonated with audiences hungry for authenticity.

In 1974, the band's lineup solidified with Tommy Ramone on drums. Tommy's engineering skills and his prior experience as a record producer played a crucial role in shaping The Ramones' sound. Under his guidance, the band recorded their eponymous debut album, "Ramones," in just a matter of days. Released in April 1976, this album was a sonic manifesto, featuring anthems like "Blitzkrieg Bop" and "I Wanna Be Your Boyfriend." It was a declaration of punk's arrival, a call to arms for a generation seeking an alternative to the mainstream.

The Ramones' emergence onto the music scene was nothing short of revolutionary. Their minimalist approach to music, characterized by three-chord simplicity and rapid-fire beats, challenged the prevailing norms of rock 'n' roll. They stripped away the excess, rejecting intricate solos and lengthy compositions in Favor of short, catchy songs that distilled the essence of rebellion.

In the wake of their debut album, The Ramones embarked on a relentless touring schedule, crisscrossing the United States and Europe. They inspired a legion of fans and musicians who were drawn to their authentic, unapologetic approach. The Ramones' impact extended far beyond their music; it was a cultural phenomenon that reshaped the course of rock history.

In retrospect, The Ramones' formation can be seen as a natural response to the zeitgeist of the 1970s. They were a reaction to the excesses of mainstream rock and a reflection of the frustrations and yearnings of a generation. The Ramones' rejection of convention, their embrace of individuality, and their uncompromising pursuit of authenticity laid the groundwork for the punk movement.

The New York City punk scene of the mid-1970s was a crucible of creativity, rebellion, and experimentation. It was a scene that not only gave birth to punk rock as a genre but also played a pivotal role in shaping The Ramones' distinctive sound and attitude, suggests Likewolf (2023). As we dive into the influence of the New York City punk scene on The Ramones' music, we uncover a melting pot of artistic expression and raw energy that fuelled the band's rise to legendary status.

At the epicentre of the New York City punk explosion was CBGB, a grungy dive bar located at 315 Bowery in Manhattan's East Village. CBGB, which stood for "Country, Bluegrass, and Blues" (though it would soon become synonymous with punk), was the beating heart of the punk scene. It was a place where the misfits, the outsiders, and the musically adventurous came to forge a new sound and defy convention.

The Ramones' association with CBGB was instrumental in defining their early sound. History.com Editors. (2021). Points out The Ramones played their first gig at CBGB on August 16, 1974, a date that would go down in punk history. CBGB's intimate and unpretentious setting provided the perfect platform for The Ramones to hone their rapid-fire, high-energy performances. Their sets were a whirlwind of short, catchy songs, often lasting no more than two minutes. It was at CBGB that The Ramones' minimalist approach to music found its home.

While CBGB was the primary punk Mecca, another legendary New York City venue, Max's Kansas City, played a different but equally influential role in The Ramones' journey. Max's was known for its association with the glam rock scene, but it also embraced punk and new wave acts. The Ramones frequently performed at Max's, and the venue exposed them to a diverse audience that included artists, musicians, and creative minds from various backgrounds.

Max's Kansas City introduced The Ramones to a broader artistic community, and the band's interactions with fellow musicians and creative individuals contributed to their unique approach. It was here that they crossed paths with artists like Andy Warhol and David Bowie, who recognized the band's potential and encouraged their artistic endeavours. These encounters broadened The Ramones' horizons and reinforced their belief that punk was not confined to a single sound or style.

The New York City punk scene was marked by a spirit of collaboration and cross-pollination. Musicians from various bands often shared bills and stages, and this intermingling of creative energies was a hallmark of the era. The Ramones, while maintaining their distinctive style, were not immune to this influence.

One of the most notable collaborations occurred between The Ramones and members of the New York Dolls. Johnny Thunders and Jerry Nolan, former members of the New York Dolls, briefly joined The Ramones in 1975, adding their own glam-punk flair to the band's lineup. While this union was short-lived, it underscored the sense of community and experimentation that defined the New York City punk scene.

Perhaps the most profound influence of the New York City punk scene on The Ramones was the spirit of defiance and individuality that permeated the movement. Punk was not just a genre; it was a rejection of the mainstream, a call to arms for those who felt alienated by the status quo. The Ramones embodied this ethos in every note they played and every lyric they sang.

Their songs often explored themes of teenage alienation, rebellion, and frustration. Tracks like "Blitzkrieg Bop" and "Now I Wanna Sniff Some Glue" were anthems of youthful defiance. The Ramones' rejection of virtuosity in Favor of raw, unfiltered energy was a direct response to the excesses of contemporary rock music. Their attitude was clear: anyone could pick up an instrument and make music; you didn't need to be a virtuoso to rock.

The Ramones' immersion in the New York City punk scene not only shaped their sound but also cemented their legacy as one of punk's most iconic bands. They were the embodiment of the city's grit and attitude, and their music resonated with a generation that was hungry for something authentic and unapologetic.

The New York City punk scene was a hotbed of creativity and rebellion, and The Ramones were at its forefront. Their enduring impact on music and popular culture can be traced back to those dingy clubs, where they honed their craft and forged a sound that defied convention. The Ramones were more than just a band; they were the torchbearers of a musical revolution that continues to influence generations of musicians and rebels around the world.

### The Cut of Their Jib

The Ramones, a pioneering punk rock band formed in the early 1970s, are renowned not only for their music but also for their distinctive fashion sense.

Their unique look, characterized by leather jackets, torn jeans, and unconventional hairstyles, played a crucial role in shaping the punk rock subculture.

First and foremost, the leather jackets worn by the band members became iconic symbols of their rebellious image. These jackets, often in classic black, were emblematic of the countercultural movements that influenced punk rock. The leather jacket conveyed an edgy and defiant attitude, aligning the Ramones with the rebellious spirit of rock 'n' roll and the biker subculture. This choice of attire was not just a fashion statement but a statement of intent, signalling their rejection of mainstream norms.

In addition to the leather jackets, the Ramones embraced torn and ripped jeans as part of their fashion repertoire. This was a bold departure from the polished and flamboyant attire of many rock bands of their time. The torn jeans reflected a do-it-yourself (DIY) ethos, as if the band members had taken scissors and razors to their pants themselves. This fashion choice symbolized a disregard for conventional fashion rules and an embrace of a raw, unpolished aesthetic.

Another key aspect of their distinctive look was their unconventional hairstyles. The Ramones sported shaggy, straight-cut, and often bowl-style haircuts that defied the prevailing norms of long, flowing locks in the rock world. These haircuts, like their clothing choices, were intentionally anti-establishment. They gave the band members an instantly recognizable appearance that reinforced their outsider status in the music industry.

The Ramones' music was as distinctive and groundbreaking as their fashion sense. At the heart of their musical style was a commitment to simplicity and speed, epitomized by their three-chord approach and short, high-energy songs.

Perhaps the most defining aspect of the Ramones' music was their three-chord approach. Most of their songs were built on a basic structure of three chords, typically played at breakneck speed. This simplicity made their music incredibly accessible, even to those with minimal musical training. It was an intentional departure from the complex and intricate compositions that dominated the rock music landscape of the time.

The brevity of Ramones songs was another striking feature. Many of their tracks lasted less than two minutes, packing a powerful punch in a short span of time. This was a departure from the long, elaborate arrangements of their contemporaries. The Ramones embraced a "get in, make a statement, and get out" philosophy, creating an urgent and intense listening experience.

The speed at which the Ramones played was electrifying. Their high-energy performances, characterized by rapid tempos and aggressive guitar work, set them apart from the more laid-back rock acts of the 1970s. This approach created an atmosphere of excitement and rebellion at their live shows, further solidifying their reputation as pioneers of punk rock. The Ramones' minimalist style and sound had a profound and lasting impact on the punk genre, influencing not only music but also the broader culture.

One of the most significant contributions of the Ramones was their embodiment of the DIY ethos. Their simplistic and accessible music, along with their anti-establishment fashion choices, encouraged a generation of fans to pick up instruments and start their own bands. This democratization of music creation helped fuel the proliferation of punk rock and alternative music scenes worldwide. The Ramones essentially gave birth to a movement that prized individualism and self-expression over technical virtuosity.

Furthermore, the Ramones' fashion choices, including leather jackets, torn jeans, and unconventional hairstyles, reshaped the punk aesthetic. These elements became synonymous with punk rock fashion, and many bands that followed in their footsteps adopted similar styles. The leather jacket, in particular, became a symbol of rebellion and outsider status, an emblematic part of punk identity.

Musically, the Ramones' minimalist style laid the foundation for punk's future development. Their straightforward three-chord approach influenced countless punk and alternative rock bands that emerged in the late 1970s and beyond. Bands like The Clash and Sex Pistols borrowed heavily from the Ramones' playbook, crafting fast, energetic, and politically charged music that defined the punk movement.

The Ramones' self-titled debut album, released in 1976, was a watershed moment in the history of punk rock. Produced by Sire Records, the album was recorded in a mere seven days, perfectly capturing the band's raw energy and minimalist approach to music. The album cover itself, featuring a black-and-white photograph of the band, clad in their signature leather jackets and torn jeans, became an iconic image of the punk movement.

The opening track, "Blitzkrieg Bop," is often considered the Ramones' anthem. Its catchy, repetitive chorus, "Hey, ho, let's go!" became a rallying cry for punk fans. The song's simple three-chord structure and breakneck speed epitomized the Ramones' musical style. "Blitzkrieg Bop" not only introduced the band to the world but also set the tone for the entire punk genre with its raw power and rebellious attitude.

Following "Blitzkrieg Bop," the album continued with a barrage of short, high-energy tracks, such as "Beat on the Brat," "Judy Is a Punk," and "Now I Wanna Sniff Some Glue." These songs were characterized by their irreverent lyrics and aggressive sound, solidifying the Ramones' status as punk pioneers. The debut album's impact was profound, serving as a blueprint for countless punk and alternative bands that followed.

Hot on the heels of their debut success, the Ramones released their second album, "Leave Home," in 1977. While retaining the same punk ethos, this album showcased the band's evolution and refinement of their signature sound.

One standout track from "Leave Home" was "I Wanna Be Sedated." This song, with its catchy melody and lyrics about seeking escape from the mundane, struck a chord with listeners. It remains one of the Ramones' most beloved and enduring hits. "I Wanna Be Sedated" exemplified the band's ability to blend pop sensibilities with punk aggression, making their music accessible to a wider audience.

"Pinhead," another track from "Leave Home," introduced the famous Ramones chant, "Gabba Gabba Hey!" This chant became a unifying slogan for punk fans and is still chanted at punk shows around the world. The Ramones' ability to create anthems and slogans contributed significantly to their cultural impact.

In 1977, the Ramones released "Rocket to Russia," their third studio album, which included the iconic track "Sheena Is a Punk Rocker." This song was a departure from some of their earlier, more abrasive material. It had a more upbeat and melodic sound, reflecting the band's versatility within the punk genre. "Sheena Is a Punk Rocker" celebrated punk culture and youth rebellion. The lyrics told the story of a punk girl named Sheena, and the song's infectious melody made it an instant classic. Its portrayal of Sheena as a symbol of punk liberation resonated with fans and encapsulated the spirit of the punk movement.

These iconic Ramones songs have left an indelible mark on both music history and popular culture. "Blitzkrieg Bop" remains a stadium and arena anthem, often played at sporting events to energize the crowd. Its inclusion in countless films, TV shows, and commercials has cemented its place in the collective consciousness. "I Wanna Be Sedated" continues to be a relatable anthem for anyone seeking an escape from the daily grind. Its enduring popularity is evidenced by its frequent use in movies, commercials, and cover versions by other artists. "Sheena Is a Punk Rocker" captured the essence of punk's rebellious spirit and is often cited as one of the quintessential punk rock songs. Its influence can be heard in the music of subsequent generations of punk and alternative rock bands.

Beyond their musical impact, these songs played a crucial role in shaping the cultural identity of the punk movement. They provided anthems for disaffected youth, rallying cries for those seeking an alternative to mainstream culture. The Ramones' music and image embodied a countercultural spirit that challenged the status quo.

The Ramones' legendary live performances were nothing short of electric, characterized by an unmatched intensity and raw energy. From the moment they stepped on stage, the band unleashed a relentless sonic assault that left audiences exhilarated and sometimes stunned. Their songs, often clocking in at under two minutes, were played at breakneck speed, creating a frenetic atmosphere that was impossible to resist. The band members, clad in their iconic leather jackets and torn jeans, exuded a rebellious charisma that drew fans into their world of punk rock defiance.

One of the most striking aspects of the Ramones' live shows was the power of brevity. In an era when rock bands often indulged in extended solos and elaborate stage theatrics, the Ramones took a minimalist approach. Their short and fast songs left no room for excess, getting straight to the point with catchy melodies and incisive lyrics. This brevity had a magnetic effect, keeping audiences engaged and hungry for more. The Ramones didn't waste a single moment on stage, packing their sets with as many songs as possible, leaving fans exhilarated and sometimes breathless by the end.

The Ramones' live performances left an indelible mark on the music industry and the punk rock subculture. Their uncompromising intensity and brevity set a new standard for live shows, influencing countless bands that followed. The Ramones demonstrated that a concert didn't need to be long and elaborate to be memorable; it could be a powerful, high-octane experience that left a lasting impression. Even today, their live recordings and concert footage serve as a testament to the enduring legacy of their performances, reminding us of the explosive energy and rebellious spirit that defined the Ramones on stage.

The Ramones' influence on the punk rock movement and subsequent generations of musicians is immeasurable. They were the catalyst for a musical revolution that challenged the status quo and redefined the very essence of rock and roll. The Ramones' stripped-down, high-energy sound and rebellious attitude shattered the conventions of 1970s rock music, and their impact rippled through the music world for decades to come.

The Ramones' legacy endures as a testament to their enduring impact on music and culture. They are revered as one of the founding pillars of punk rock, and their influence can be heard in the music of countless bands across genres, from punk and alternative to indie rock and beyond.

In the pantheon of punk rock icons, The Ramones occupy a place of unmatched significance. Their contribution to the genre's development and global dissemination is unparalleled. They not only pioneered a musical style but also embodied the punk ethos, championing individualism, anti-establishment values, and the do-it-yourself spirit.

Their cultural resonance extends beyond music, as they symbolize a countercultural movement that transcends generations. The Ramones continue to inspire artists who seek to challenge the mainstream and embrace their authentic selves. Their legacy serves as a reminder that music is a powerful tool for social change and self-expression.

In the annals of music history, The Ramones stand as a symbol of rebellion and authenticity. Their music and style became a rallying point for generations of fans who rejected conformity and celebrated individualism. Their impact on the punk rock movement and subsequent generations of musicians cannot be overstated. The Ramones' enduring legacy as punk rock icons continues to inspire artists to this day, reminding us that the spirit of punk lives on through those who dare to challenge the norm, embrace simplicity, and rock with unbridled intensity. In the grand tapestry of music, The Ramones are an essential thread, forever woven into the fabric of punk rock's DNA.

# DIVISION.2-2

## UK Anarchists

In the tumultuous landscape of the 1970s music scene, one band emerged from the heart of London with a roar that would forever change the face of rock 'n' roll. The Sex Pistols, with their explosive energy, anarchic ethos, and confrontational style, became the standard-bearers of punk rock, an irreverent and rebellious movement that challenged the musical establishment and societal norms.

This division explores the rise, impact, and enduring legacy of the Sex Pistols, a band that left an indelible mark on music, fashion, and culture. From their contentious debut single "Anarchy in the UK" to their provocative and audacious album "Never Mind the Bollocks, Here's the Sex Pistols," we delve into the band's tumultuous journey through punk's tumultuous landscape. We also examine the tragic events that surrounded bassist Sid Vicious and discuss the band's cultural significance, from their fearless fashion sense to their uncompromising attitude.

Join us as we dive headfirst into the maelstrom of punk rebellion with the Sex Pistols, a band that defined an era, shook the foundations of the music industry, and ignited a fire of dissent that still burns brightly in the hearts of those who dare to challenge the status quo.

## Before the Bollocks Drop

In the smoky, dimly lit clubs of 1970s London, a band was taking shape that would soon set the world ablaze with its raw energy and unapologetic rebellion. The Sex Pistols, a name that would become synonymous with punk rock, had its humble beginnings as a group known as "The Strand." This section delves into the band's early formation, the lineup changes that shaped its identity, and the trials and tribulations faced by these young rebels in search of their musical calling.

The year was 1972, and the British music scene was undergoing a transformation. Glam rock was at its peak, and the airwaves were filled with flamboyant acts like T. Rex and David Bowie. In the midst of this musical landscape, three young friends—Steve Jones, Paul Cook, and Wally Nightingale—decided to form a band. This nascent group, initially known as "The Strand," had no grand aspirations at the time. They were just kids from Shepherd's Bush, drawn together by a shared love for rock 'n' roll.

"The Strand" began playing in small, local venues, testing their musical mettle in a city teeming with aspiring musicians. While their early performances showed glimpses of potential, they were still a long way from the punk revolution that lay ahead. The band's sound at this stage was somewhat directionless, a mix of rock covers and experimentation. They hadn't yet found their distinctive voice, but the seeds of rebellion were sown, waiting for the right catalyst to ignite their punk spirit.

## Something's Rotten in the "The Strand" of England

THE TURNING POINT FOR "The Strand" came in the form of a scrappy and outspoken young man named John Lydon, who would soon adopt the stage name Johnny Rotten. Lydon, with his shock of bright orange hair and confrontational attitude, brought a new dimension to the band. He wasn't just a singer; he was a provocateur, a disruptor of the norm.

Lydon's arrival in the band marked a shift in their trajectory. His abrasive charisma and disdain for the establishment would become the driving force behind the Sex Pistols' rebellion. It was under Lydon's influence that the band embraced punk as not just a musical genre but a cultural and political statement. The name "Sex Pistols" was chosen to shock and provoke, a reflection of their newfound ethos.

### Matlock and Future Gary Oldman

With Johnny Rotten at the helm, the Sex Pistols were still in need of a solid rhythm section to complete their lineup. This is when two more key figures entered the picture: Sid Vicious and Glen Matlock. Sid Vicious, with his wild appearance and chaotic energy, would eventually become the band's bassist. His persona perfectly encapsulated the punk rebellion that the Sex Pistols embodied.

Glen Matlock, on the other hand, joined as the band's bassist initially, playing a crucial role in shaping the band's early sound. His melodic sensibilities and songwriting skills contributed to the band's early material. However, Matlock's departure from the band in 1977 marked a significant change in the Sex Pistols' lineup. He was replaced by Sid Vicious, whose turbulent presence added to the band's volatile image.

### Prepubescence

As the Sex Pistols began to solidify their lineup, they faced the challenges that often accompany a burgeoning punk band. They played in dingy venues and squats, performing for audiences who were often more perplexed than impressed by their confrontational style. Financial struggles were a constant companion, with the band members often scraping together meagre sums to fund their musical endeavours.

Musically, the Sex Pistols were in a state of flux during their early years. They experimented with different styles, attempting to find their sonic identity. It wasn't until they embraced the raw, aggressive sound that would become punk rock that they truly found their footing. The band's determination to break free from convention and their unapologetic rejection of the mainstream set the stage for their explosive rise as icons of punk rebellion.

The formation and early years of the Sex Pistols were marked by evolution, experimentation, and the arrival of key members who would shape the band's identity. From their humble beginnings as "The Strand" to the transformation brought about by Johnny Rotten, Sid Vicious, and Glen Matlock, the Sex Pistols were on a collision course with punk rock history. Their early struggles and musical exploration laid the foundation for the punk revolution that was about to unfold, challenging the status quo and setting the stage for their legendary rebellion.

### The Bollocks Drop

In the autumn of 1976, the British music scene was on the brink of a seismic shift. The Sex Pistols, a band of provocateurs and rebels from the gritty streets of London, were about to unleash a musical Molotov cocktail that would set the stage for the explosive rise of punk rock in the United Kingdom. At the centre of this revolution was their debut single, "Anarchy in the UK."

Released on November 26, 1976, "Anarchy in the UK" was the Sex Pistols' inaugural assault on the music establishment. From its opening chords to Johnny Rotten's snarling vocals, the song was a declaration of rebellion and a call to arms for a disenchanted youth. "I am an Antichrist, I am an anarchist," proclaimed Rotten in the opening lines, leaving no room for subtlety. The lyrics were a direct challenge to the status quo, a rejection of conformity, and an embrace of chaos and dissent.

Musically, "Anarchy in the UK" was a revelation. It combined the aggression of punk with a raw, unpolished sound that was a stark departure from the slick and orchestrated rock of the era. The driving guitar riffs, thundering bassline, and relentless drumming created a sonic assault that demanded attention. It was clear that the Sex Pistols were not here to play by the rules, and "Anarchy in the UK" was the anthem that signalled their arrival.

At the heart of "Anarchy in the UK" was a rebellious attitude that resonated with disaffected youth across the country. The song's lyrics encapsulated the frustration and disillusionment of a generation that felt alienated by the political and social climate of 1970s Britain. It was an era marked by economic recession, high unemployment, and a sense of stagnation, and the Sex Pistols were the musical embodiment of this discontent.

Johnny Rotten's delivery was confrontational and unapologetic. His snide and sneering vocals, backed by the band's explosive energy, captured the spirit of rebellion. The refrain, "I wanna destroy the passerby," was a declaration of war against the establishment and an invitation to join the ranks of those who rejected the status quo. "Anarchy in the UK" was a rallying cry for anyone who felt marginalized or voiceless, offering a sense of empowerment through its unrelenting defiance.

The release of "Anarchy in the UK" catapulted the Sex Pistols into the national spotlight, but it was a fateful television interview that would turn them into household names and fuel a media firestorm. On December 1, 1976, the Sex Pistols appeared on the "Today" show hosted by Bill Grundy. What transpired during this interview would become the stuff of legend and infamy.

From the outset, the interview was tense and confrontational. The band members, led by Johnny Rotten, used profanity and engaged in provocative banter that shocked viewers and appalled the show's producers. The most infamous moment came when Steve Jones, the band's guitarist, directed a profanity-laden tirade at Grundy himself. The interview descended into chaos, with Grundy goading the band members to continue their provocative behaviour.

The fallout from the interview was immediate and intense. The Sex Pistols were dropped from their record label, EMI, as a result of the controversy. Yet, paradoxically, this controversy propelled the band to even greater notoriety. It seemed that the more the establishment tried to suppress them, the more the Sex Pistols thrived on the rebellion and anti-authoritarian image that had become their trademark.

"Anarchy in the UK" was more than just a song; it was a cultural detonation that reverberated throughout the UK and beyond. Its provocative lyrics and rebellious attitude resonated with a generation that was hungry for change and a voice to express their frustrations. The media frenzy and controversy that surrounded the Sex Pistols, particularly the Bill Grundy interview, catapulted them to notoriety and solidified their status as punk icons.

The song itself became an anthem of defiance, a soundtrack for a youth rebellion that rejected the establishment and sought to tear down the old order. "Anarchy in the UK" marked the birth of punk rock as a cultural force, and its impact can still be felt in the music, fashion, and attitude of subsequent generations. The Sex Pistols had ignited a revolution, and "Anarchy in the UK" was the incendiary spark that set the punk rock explosion ablaze.

### Never Mind the Bollocks: Album Number 1... out of 1

In the annals of punk rock history, few albums carry as much weight and provocation as "Never Mind the Bollocks, Here's the Sex Pistols." Released in 1977, this incendiary album marked a pivotal moment in the evolution of punk music, society, and culture. This analysis delves into the creation and release of the Sex Pistols' only studio album, examining its significance within punk rock history, the confrontational title, and the cultural and musical impact of standout tracks like "God Save the Queen" and "Anarchy in the UK."

In the midst of the late 1970s punk explosion, the Sex Pistols were poised to unleash their debut studio album, a release that would capture the essence of the movement and etch their name into music history. The creation of "Never Mind the Bollocks, Here's the Sex Pistols" was a tumultuous journey fraught with challenges, yet it would ultimately become the quintessential punk rock manifesto.

The album was recorded between March and August of 1977 at Wessex Studios in London, under the production guidance of Chris Thomas. During these sessions, the Sex Pistols—Johnny Rotten (vocals), Steve Jones (guitar), Sid

Vicious (bass), and Paul Cook (drums)—poured their pent-up aggression, irreverence, and social discontent into the music. The result was a collection of tracks that encapsulated the spirit of rebellion, captured in a visceral, unfiltered sound.

From the moment the album was announced, it courted controversy with its provocative title, "Never Mind the Bollocks, Here's the Sex Pistols." The use of the word "bollocks," a British slang term for testicles, was seen as a deliberate affront to decency and societal norms. The title was a brazen middle finger to censorship, and it defiantly challenged the establishment's authority over language and expression. In doing so, it perfectly encapsulated the band's ethos of confrontation and rebellion.

The album's cover art, designed by Jamie Reid, further emphasized its confrontational stance. It featured a stark image of a bright yellow background with block letters spelling out the album's title, disrupted by holes cut through the letters. The bold design was a visual representation of the Sex Pistols' desire to tear through convention and established norms. It was an album cover that demanded attention and challenged the observer, much like the music contained within.

One of the standout tracks on the album, "God Save the Queen," was a direct affront to the monarchy and a scathing critique of British society. Released during the Silver Jubilee of Queen Elizabeth II, the song's lyrics declared, "God save the queen, she ain't no human being." This inflammatory line not only criticized the monarchy but also questioned the deification of the queen in British society.

Musically, "God Save the Queen" was a punk rock anthem of dissent. The driving guitar riffs, Johnny Rotten's sneering vocals, and the relentless drumming created an atmosphere of rebellion and outrage. The song's defiant energy struck a chord with a generation disillusioned with the status quo, leading it to become an unofficial anthem of the punk movement.

"Anarchy in the UK," the track that had previously served as the Sex Pistols' introduction to the world, also found its place on the album. This song, with its confrontational lyrics and aggressive sound, had already established itself as a punk rock classic. However, its inclusion on "Never Mind the Bollocks" solidified its status as an essential punk anthem.

The song's opening line, "I am an Antichrist, I am an anarchist," was a rallying cry for those who rejected the establishment and sought to tear down the old order. Musically, "Anarchy in the UK" was a relentless onslaught of punk energy, featuring Steve Jones's iconic guitar work and Johnny Rotten's snarling vocals. The song's enduring appeal lies in its ability to capture the raw, rebellious spirit of punk, making it a timeless anthem of defiance.

"Never Mind the Bollocks, Here's the Sex Pistols" left an indelible mark on both punk rock and popular culture. Its confrontational title and provocative lyrics challenged the boundaries of expression and freedom of speech. The album served as a rallying point for a generation of disillusioned youth who sought to challenge the establishment and redefine the norms of society.

Musically, the album's impact was equally profound. It helped solidify the punk rock sound, characterized by its raw, unpolished energy and defiant attitude. The Sex Pistols' aggressive approach to music inspired countless bands in the punk and alternative rock genres, shaping the course of music history.

"Never Mind the Bollocks, Here's the Sex Pistols" was more than an album; it was a cultural detonation. Its confrontational title, provocative lyrics, and unfiltered sound challenged the status quo and ignited a revolution in music and society. Tracks like "God Save the Queen" and "Anarchy in the UK" became anthems of dissent and rebellion, leaving an enduring legacy that continues to inspire generations of musicians and rebels who dare to challenge the established order.

As the tumultuous journey of the Sex Pistols continued, the band found itself increasingly embroiled in chaos and conflict. The internal tensions, fuelled by substance abuse, personal differences, and the relentless media scrutiny, had reached a boiling point. Johnny Rotten, the band's enigmatic frontman, had grown disenchanted with the infighting and the negative publicity that seemed to overshadow their music. The ill-fated U.S. tour in January 1978 proved to be the breaking point. Concerts were cancelled, and the band's reputation was tarnished as they navigated a barrage of controversies. Amid the mayhem, Rotten made the fateful announcement: the Sex Pistols were officially disbanded. The meteoric rise and abrupt fall of the Sex Pistols, marked by their confrontational attitude and relentless rebellion, had reached its dramatic conclusion, leaving a void in the punk rock landscape that would resonate for generations to come.

In January 1978, the band officially disbanded. The chaos that had surrounded their brief but meteoric career had taken its toll. Johnny Rotten, the band's iconic frontman, had grown disillusioned with the infighting, drug abuse, and negative publicity that had become synonymous with the Sex Pistols. He announced the band's breakup during their ill-fated U.S. tour.

The dissolution of the Sex Pistols marked the end of an era, but it also solidified their status as punk icons. Despite their short-lived existence, the band had left an indelible mark on music history. Their confrontational attitude, raw energy, and unapologetic rebellion had reshaped the punk rock landscape, inspiring countless bands and defining the genre's ethos.

### A Vicious Tragedy

In the annals of punk rock history, few stories are as fraught with turmoil, tragedy, and tumult as that of Sid Vicious, the notorious bassist of the Sex Pistols. His brief but impactful tenure in the band, his tumultuous relationship with Nancy Spungen, and the tragic events that unfolded would leave an indelible mark on the punk scene, and rock 'n' roll history. This exploration delves into the life and times of Sid Vicious, the ill-fated love affair with Nancy Spungen, and the grim circumstances that led to her death and Vicious's subsequent arrest. We also examine the profound impact of these events on the Sex Pistols and the broader punk rock community.

In 1977, the Sex Pistols were in the midst of a whirlwind rise to infamy. Their confrontational music and unapologetic rebellion had propelled them into the spotlight of the punk rock movement. But beneath the surface, tensions within the band were brewing, and the arrival of Sid Vicious would prove to be a catalyst for both creativity and chaos.

Sid Vicious, born John Ritchie, joined the Sex Pistols as their bassist in early 1977, replacing Glen Matlock. His persona was emblematic of punk's rebellious spirit, with a shock of black hair, torn clothes, and a penchant for self-destruction. Although he wasn't initially a skilled musician, his wild energy and unbridled enthusiasm endeared him to the band and their fans. Vicious quickly became an iconic figure in the punk scene, embodying the anti-establishment ethos that the Sex Pistols represented.

It wasn't long before Sid Vicious's life became entangled with Nancy Spungen's, a relationship that would become synonymous with punk rock excess and tragedy. Nancy, an American expatriate with her own history of mental health struggles, addiction, and tumultuous relationships, became Vicious's girlfriend and muse. Their relationship was marked by a toxic combination of drug abuse, violence, and co-dependency, and it soon spiralled into a chaotic and destructive affair.

The presence of Nancy Spungen had a profound impact on the band and Sid Vicious himself. While the Sex Pistols had always courted controversy, Vicious and Spungen's relationship intensified the media scrutiny and fascination surrounding the band. The image of Sid and Nancy, often referred to as the "Bonnie and Clyde of punk," embodied the nihilistic excess and self-destructive tendencies of punk rock in its rawest form.

The climax of this tumultuous relationship came on the night of October 12, 1978, at the Chelsea Hotel in New York City. Nancy Spungen was found dead in the bathroom of the hotel, the victim of a fatal stab wound. Sid Vicious was arrested and charged with her murder, and released on bail. Four months later he would be found dead of a drug overdose.

The circumstances surrounding Nancy's death remain shrouded in mystery and controversy. Some believe that it was a drug-fuelled domestic dispute that ended in tragedy, while others speculate about the involvement of other parties. Regardless of the details, the incident marked a dark chapter in punk rock history, one that underscored the self-destructive tendencies that had come to define the genre. The incident also cast a shadow over the punk movement itself. Punk had always been an anti-establishment and confrontational subculture, but the media frenzy surrounding Sid and Nancy's tragic end painted punk rock as a nihilistic and dangerous movement. Punk was suddenly seen as a menace to society, and the subculture faced increased scrutiny and criticism.

The tumultuous tenure of Sid Vicious, his ill-fated relationship with Nancy Spungen, and the tragic events that unfolded were a dark and tragic chapter in the history of punk rock. Their story serves as a cautionary tale of excess, self-destruction, and the toll that fame and addiction can take on even the most iconic figures.

The impact of these events on the Sex Pistols and the punk scene as a whole cannot be understated. The band's dissolution marked the end of a legendary era in punk, while also cementing their status as punk icons. The legacy of Sid Vicious and Nancy Spungen, for better or worse, remains intertwined with the punk rock ethos of rebellion and nonconformity, serving as a stark reminder of the destructive forces that can lurk beneath the surface of artistic expression and cultural rebellion.

### Short Lived with an Eternal Influence

The Sex Pistols, in their brief and turbulent existence, left an indelible mark on music, fashion, and pop culture. Their legacy extends far beyond their time in the spotlight, transcending the boundaries of punk rock and shaping the cultural landscape for generations. This examination delves into the lasting impact of the Sex Pistols on various facets of society, including their role in challenging societal norms and the establishment, their influence on subsequent punk and alternative rock bands, and their significant contributions to the punk aesthetic, including DIY fashion and rebellious imagery.

Their impact extended beyond music, as they challenged the very fabric of British culture. The band's confrontations with the media and establishment figures, such as the infamous interview with Bill Grundy, served to galvanize a new generation of youth who were disillusioned with the status quo. The Sex Pistols didn't just play music; they were agents of social upheaval who paved the way for a new era of cultural rebellion.

The Sex Pistols were more than a band; they were a force of nature that reshaped the musical landscape. Their raw and aggressive sound, characterized by short, explosive songs driven by Steve Jones's guitar riffs and Johnny Rotten's snarling vocals, set the template for punk rock. Countless bands that followed, from The Clash and Buzzcocks to Ramones and Dead Kennedys, drew inspiration from the Sex Pistols' sonic intensity and DIY ethos.

Perhaps one of the most significant aspects of the Sex Pistols' influence on subsequent bands was their unwavering commitment to authenticity. They showed the world that punk wasn't about technical proficiency; it was about passion and attitude. This message resonated with legions of young musicians who, armed with little more than a guitar and a desire to rebel, formed their own bands and took to the stage. The punk and alternative rock movements that followed were a testament to the Sex Pistols' enduring influence.

In particular, the do-it-yourself (DIY) ethos championed by the Sex Pistols became a guiding principle for punk and alternative musicians. They demonstrated that you didn't need expensive equipment or formal training to make music; all you needed was a voice and a willingness to express yourself. This democratization of music creation opened the door for countless underground bands to emerge and challenge the mainstream.

Beyond their music, the Sex Pistols played a pivotal role in shaping the punk aesthetic, a visual language that mirrored their rebellious spirit. The band's fashion choices, characterized by torn clothes, provocative slogans, and defiant hairstyles, became synonymous with punk rock. They weren't just musicians; they were walking statements of nonconformity.

DIY fashion, in particular, was a hallmark of punk culture, and the Sex Pistols embodied this ethos. They encouraged their fans to reject consumerism and create their own clothing, often emblazoned with politically charged slogans and band logos. This punk fashion rebellion rejected the idea that style should be dictated by the fashion industry and instead celebrated individualism and self-expression.

The Sex Pistols' album art and imagery further reinforced their rebellious message. Jamie Reid's iconic artwork for "Never Mind the Bollocks, Here's the Sex Pistols," with its bold design and defiant cut-out letters, challenged conventional album covers and served as a visual manifesto for punk rock. This imagery, combined with provocative stage performances, created an unforgettable aesthetic that resonated with fans and forever altered the visual landscape of rock music.

The Sex Pistols' impact on music, fashion, and pop culture endures as a testament to their uncompromising rebellion. They challenged societal norms and the establishment with their confrontational music and attitude, leaving an indelible mark on punk rock and influencing subsequent generations of musicians. Their contributions to the punk aesthetic, particularly in DIY fashion and rebellious imagery, continue to inspire artists who seek to challenge the mainstream and embrace their authentic selves. The Sex Pistols' legacy is a reminder that the spirit of punk lives on through those who dare to challenge the norm, reject conformity, and rock with unbridled intensity.

# DIVISION.2-3

### Titans of The Clash

IN THE LATE 1970S, amidst the gritty streets and cultural upheaval of London, a musical revolution was brewing. It was a time of social unrest, economic turmoil, and a generation of disenchanted youth searching for an outlet to voice their frustrations. In the midst of this tumultuous landscape, The Clash was born. This section delves into the origins of The Clash in London in 1976, exploring the band's early lineup and key members, their formative influences, and the vibrant punk scene that would shape their distinctive sound.

The story of The Clash begins in the summer of 1976 when two musicians from contrasting backgrounds crossed paths in the heart of London. Joe Strummer, a charismatic frontman with a passion for political activism, joined forces with Mick Jones, a guitarist steeped in rock 'n' roll and rhythm and blues. The duo's chemistry was palpable, and they quickly realized they were onto something significant.

The initial lineup of The Clash was a reflection of the eclectic and diverse musical landscape of London at the time. Joining Strummer and Jones were Paul Simonon, a bassist and artist known for his striking visuals, and Terry Chimes on drums. This lineup laid the foundation for what would become one of the most influential bands in rock history.

### Joe Strummer

Born John Graham Mellor, Joe Strummer adopted his stage name as a nod to his tumultuous teenage years. He was the band's lead vocalist and rhythm guitarist, known for his distinctive gravelly voice and politically charged lyrics. Strummer's fervent commitment to social justice and activism would become a defining characteristic of The Clash.

### Mick Jones

Mick Jones, the band's lead guitarist and co-lead vocalist, brought a keen sense of melody and an appreciation for various musical styles, from punk to reggae. His songwriting partnership with Strummer was central to The Clash's creative force.

### Paul Simonon

Paul Simonon, the band's bassist, was not only the anchor of the rhythm section but also a visual artist responsible for some of The Clash's iconic imagery. His cool demeanour and artistic sensibilities added a unique dimension to the band's identity.

### Topper Headon

Initially Terry Chimes, then later replaced by Topper Headon on drums, provided the band's driving rhythms. Topper's addition solidified The Clash's classic lineup and contributed to their distinctive sound.

## The Clash

The Clash's sound was a reflection of their eclectic musical influences and inspirations. While punk rock was at the core of their identity, their music incorporated a wide range of styles, including rock 'n' roll, reggae, ska, and rhythm and blues. This musical diversity set them apart from their punk contemporaries and contributed to their enduring appeal.

The band's early influences were the energy and rebelliousness of punk rock pioneers like the Ramones and the Sex Pistols. The Clash shared the punk ethos of challenging the establishment and breaking musical boundaries. Yet, they also drew inspiration from artists like Bob Marley and Lee "Scratch" Perry, embracing the politically charged messages and rhythms of reggae. The Clash's willingness to experiment with different genres and their commitment to musical innovation allowed them to bridge the gap between punk and mainstream rock. Their eclectic approach appealed to a broad audience, making them accessible to fans of various musical tastes.

To understand The Clash's sound, it's crucial to consider the punk scene in London during the late 1970s. London was a hotbed of creativity and rebellion, with clubs like the Roxy and the 100 Club serving as incubators for punk bands. The Clash, along with contemporaries like the Sex Pistols, The Damned, and The Buzzcocks, were at the forefront of this burgeoning movement.

The punk scene in London was defined by a do-it-yourself (DIY) ethos, a rejection of the musical establishment, and a desire to challenge societal norms. The Clash embodied these principles. Their early performances at venues like the Roxy were explosive and chaotic, capturing the raw energy and youthful rebellion of the punk movement. The Clash's sound was a reflection of the urban landscape and social climate of London. Their lyrics explored themes of unemployment, urban decay, and political disillusionment, offering a voice to the disenfranchised youth of the city. Songs like "White Riot" and "London's

Burning" were anthems of rebellion that resonated with the disaffected youth of London's suburbs.

In April 1977, The Clash unleashed their eponymous debut album upon the world. It was a raw and explosive statement of intent that immediately catapulted the band to the forefront of the punk rock scene. Produced by Mickey Foote, this album was a gritty manifestation of the frustration and disillusionment felt by the youth of late '70s Britain. Songs like "Janie Jones," "White Riot," and "Career Opportunities" were blistering anthems of rebellion, capturing the zeitgeist of punk's confrontational attitude. The Clash's socially conscious lyrics, accompanied by Joe Strummer's distinctive snarl, gave a voice to a generation disenfranchised by unemployment and political disillusionment.

The impact of The Clash's debut album on the punk scene was seismic. It challenged the status quo, inspiring countless young musicians to pick up instruments and raise their voices against the establishment. With their unrelenting energy and rebellious spirit, The Clash were instrumental in defining punk rock as a cultural force that transcended music.

While The Clash was firmly rooted in punk, their willingness to explore diverse musical influences set them apart from their contemporaries. They recognized that punk's spirit of rebellion could be channelled through various musical forms, and this experimentation began to shape their distinctive sound.

One of the most significant departures was their embrace of reggae music. In 1977, The Clash released the single "Police and Thieves," a cover of Junior Murvin's reggae classic. This marked the beginning of their exploration of reggae rhythms, which would become a defining element of their sound. Songs like "Guns of Brixton" and "Bankrobber" showcased their affinity for reggae's laid-back grooves and politically charged lyrics.

The Clash's foray into rockabilly was evident in tracks like "Brand New Cadillac," highlighting their ability to infuse punk with the rebellious spirit of early rock 'n' roll. The influence of ska music also crept into their repertoire, as heard in songs like "Rudie Can't Fail" from the seminal "London Calling" album. The Clash's eclectic taste in music transformed their sound into a melting pot of genres, setting them on a path of constant musical evolution.

With their second album, "Give 'Em Enough Rope," The Clash continued to evolve their sound. Released in 1978, this album marked a departure from the rawness of their debut. Produced by Sandy Pearlman, it showcased a more polished and refined sound while maintaining the band's signature intensity.

"Give 'Em Enough Rope" demonstrated The Clash's lyrical growth, as seen in songs like "Safe European Home" and "Stay Free," which explored themes of travel, self-discovery, and personal reflection. While the album didn't enjoy the same critical acclaim as their debut, it represented a band that was maturing both musically and lyrically. However, it's important to note that "Give 'Em Enough Rope" was not without its controversies and tensions within the band. The production process was marred by clashes between the band and Pearlman, reflecting the band's determination to assert creative control.

In December 1979, The Clash released an album that would not only redefine their sound but also alter the course of rock music history. "London Calling" was a genre-defying masterpiece that captured the zeitgeist of the late '70s and early '80s.

This double album, produced by Guy Stevens, was a sonic tour de force. It fused punk with an array of genres, including rock, reggae, ska, and even a touch of rockabilly. The Clash's willingness to experiment and break down musical barriers was on full display. Songs like the title track, "London Calling," were anthems of a generation grappling with social and political upheaval.

"London Calling" was a critical and commercial success, earning widespread acclaim for its lyrical depth, musical innovation, and emotional resonance. It transcended punk rock, showcasing The Clash as a band unafraid to explore new horizons while staying true to their roots. The album's cover art, an homage to Elvis Presley's self-titled debut, featured Paul Simonon smashing his bass guitar—a powerful image that symbolized the band's rebellion and reinvention.

Beyond their seminal albums, The Clash's evolving sound was evident in their willingness to push boundaries. They ventured into dub music with tracks like "The Crooked Beat" and "One More Time," experimenting with studio techniques that added depth and texture to their sound. Their exploration of world music also became apparent with songs like "The Magnificent Seven," where funk and rap elements were woven into their punk fabric. The Clash's live performances were a testament to their musical versatility, often featuring extended improvisations and jam sessions.

This willingness to evolve musically, to incorporate diverse influences, and to challenge the conventions of punk rock demonstrated The Clash's commitment to artistic growth and innovation. They never allowed themselves to be confined by a single genre, and in doing so, they continued to inspire countless musicians to explore the boundless possibilities of music.

Upon its release, "London Calling" received widespread critical acclaim, with many considering it one of the greatest albums in rock history. Its eclectic and genre-blurring nature appealed to a broad audience, from punk purists to mainstream music enthusiasts. Rolling Stone magazine ranked it among the top albums of all time by McCabe, S, (2020). and it earned a place in the Grammy Hall of Fame.

Commercially, "London Calling" was a success, reaching audiences far beyond the punk scene. It showcased The Clash's ability to bridge the gap between underground music and the mainstream. The album's chart success and critical acclaim solidified their status as one of the most influential bands of their generation.

The Clash's musical evolution was a testament to their willingness to push boundaries and challenge the conventions of punk rock. From their explosive debut album that ignited the punk scene to their genre-defying masterpiece "London Calling," The Clash's journey was one of constant innovation and experimentation. Their ability to embrace diverse musical influences while staying true to their rebellious spirit set them apart as pioneers of punk and icons of musical evolution.

The Clash, more than just a rock band, were torchbearers of social consciousness and political engagement in the turbulent landscape of late 20th-century Britain. This section delves into the band's politically charged lyrics and their unwavering commitment to addressing critical issues such as unemployment, racism, and social inequality. We explore emblematic songs like "White Riot," "Clampdown," and "The Guns of Brixton" as vivid examples of their political messaging and examine The Clash's active involvement in various activist causes and benefit concerts.

At the heart of The Clash's identity was their unapologetic stance on pressing societal issues. Their lyrics were more than words; they were a rallying cry for change and a reflection of the world around them. In a genre often associated with rebellion and anti-establishment sentiment, The Clash stood out for the depth and substance of their political messaging.

### "White Riot": A Call for Racial Equality

Released in 1977 on their debut album, "The Clash," "White Riot" was a powerful anthem that tackled issues of racial inequality head-on. The song's chorus, "White riot, I wanna riot; white riot, a riot of my own," was a provocative call for white youth to join the fight for racial equality, echoing the energy of the civil rights movement. It was a bold statement that challenged the complacency of white society and urged individuals to confront their privilege.

### "Clampdown": A Critique of Corporate Conformity

From their 1979 album "London Calling," "Clampdown" examined the loss of youthful idealism and the lure of corporate conformity. The song decried the dilution of individuality and the stifling of creativity in the face of societal pressures. Lines like "Let fury have the hour, anger can be power" urged listeners to resist conformity and find their voices.

### "The Guns of Brixton": A Cry Against Injustice

Written and sung by bassist Paul Simonon, "The Guns of Brixton" was a stark portrayal of racial tensions and social inequality in London's Brixton neighbourhood. Released on the "London Calling" album, the song captured the anger and frustration of marginalized communities. With lyrics like "When they kick out your front door, how you gonna come? With your hands on your head or on the trigger of your gun," it was a haunting reminder of the consequences of systemic injustice.

---

THE CLASH WERE UNAFRAID to confront the pressing issues of their time, channelling their frustrations and observations into their music. Unemployment was a pervasive issue in late '70s Britain, and it found expression in songs like "Career Opportunities," which sarcastically explored the grim prospects facing British youth.

Racism was another issue that The Clash tackled head-on, particularly evident in "White Riot" and "Guns of Brixton." These songs were not just expressions of solidarity; they were demands for change and justice. The band's willingness to use their platform to address racism resonated with audiences who shared their concerns.

Social inequality, a recurring theme in their lyrics, was also addressed in "Clampdown" and "Career Opportunities." The Clash recognized the widening gap between the haves and the have-nots and urged listeners to question the prevailing power structures.

In 1978, they participated in the "Rock Against Racism" concert in London's Victoria Park, a landmark event that sought to unite people of all backgrounds against racial prejudice. The Clash's performance was a testament to their commitment to racial equality.

They also organized and headlined the "Rock Against Racism" carnival in 1979, drawing thousands of supporters in a demonstration of unity against racism. The event featured an eclectic lineup of bands and artists from diverse backgrounds, emphasizing the power of music as a force for social change.

Benefit concerts, such as the "Jobs for Change" concert in 1984, showcased The Clash's dedication to addressing unemployment and social inequality. The band used these platforms to raise awareness and funds for causes that aligned with their values.

The Clash's activism wasn't limited to the stage. They were actively involved in political movements and campaigns, leveraging their influence to amplify the voices of marginalized communities. Their commitment to social justice was unwavering and left an indelible mark on their legacy.

The Clash's impact extended far beyond the realm of music. Their politically charged lyrics and social consciousness served as a catalyst for change and an inspiration to countless individuals. Through songs like "White Riot," "Clampdown," and "The Guns of Brixton," they challenged societal norms and gave voice to the disenfranchised.

Their activism and engagement with critical issues such as unemployment, racism, and social inequality demonstrated a band that understood the power of their platform and used it to effect change. The Clash's legacy is a reminder that music has the capacity to transcend entertainment and become a force for social justice and progress. They were not just a band; they were advocates for a better world, and their message continues to resonate today.

### The Clash's Impact on Punk and Beyond

The Clash's impact on the world of music and culture is immeasurable. They weren't just a band; they were a force of nature, a catalyst for change, and an embodiment of the punk rock ethos. In this section, we explore The Clash's pivotal role in defining the punk rock movement, their profound influence on subsequent punk and alternative rock bands, their lasting impact on music, fashion, and political activism, and how they successfully bridged the gap between punk and mainstream rock.

In the mid-1970s, punk rock was a raw, rebellious, and countercultural movement emerging from the streets of New York and London. The Clash, hailing from the latter, played an instrumental role in shaping the genre's defining characteristics. They were the embodiment of punk's do-it-yourself (DIY) ethos, a rejection of the musical establishment, and a desire to challenge societal norms.

The band's self-titled debut album in 1977 was a declaration of punk's arrival. With tracks like "White Riot," "I'm So Bored with the USA," and "Career Opportunities," The Clash encapsulated the frustrations and disillusionment of British youth. Their music was fast, aggressive, and charged with political and social commentary.

Joe Strummer's distinctive snarl and Mick Jones's incendiary guitar riffs became the anthems of a generation. The Clash's lyrics addressed unemployment, racial tension, and political disenchantment, reflecting the harsh realities of late 1970s Britain. In doing so, they gave punk rock a socially conscious edge that set them apart.

The Clash's influence on subsequent punk and alternative rock bands is undeniable. They served as a blueprint for aspiring musicians, demonstrating that punk was not merely a musical genre but a platform for social commentary and rebellion.

The Ramones may have ignited the punk flame, but The Clash fuelled its intensity. Bands like The Sex Pistols, Dead Kennedys, and The Damned were inspired by The Clash's energy, political consciousness, and unapologetic rebellion. The Clash's impact on punk's second wave and the emergence of hardcore punk cannot be overstated.

Beyond punk, The Clash's legacy extended to alternative rock and even mainstream music. Their ability to blend diverse musical influences, from reggae to rockabilly, set a precedent for bands like R.E.M., The Smiths, and U2. These bands adopted The Clash's ethos of pushing boundaries and addressing social issues through music.

The Clash's influence extended far beyond the realm of music. They were pioneers in merging music with fashion and activism, suggests Wyatt, C. (2023). Their iconic imagery, exemplified by Paul Simonon's smashing bass guitar on the "London Calling" album cover, became emblematic of punk rock.

Fashion played a significant role in The Clash's identity. Their DIY aesthetic, characterized by leather jackets, ripped jeans, and combat boots, inspired countless punk enthusiasts. The Clash weren't just performers; they were style icons who transcended music and infiltrated fashion subcultures.

In the realm of activism, The Clash were tireless advocates for change. They used their platform to address issues like racial inequality, unemployment, and social injustice. Benefit concerts and activist causes were an integral part of their agenda. Their involvement in the Rock Against Racism movement and benefit concerts for causes like Jobs for Change showcased their commitment to effecting social change through music.

One of The Clash's most remarkable achievements was their ability to bridge the gap between punk and mainstream rock. While they remained steadfast in their punk roots, their music evolved and matured. Nowhere is this more evident than in their groundbreaking album "London Calling." A genre-defying masterpiece. It seamlessly fused punk with a myriad of musical influences, including rock, reggae, ska, and rockabilly. The Clash's willingness to experiment and break down musical barriers attracted a broad audience, from punk purists to mainstream listeners.

"London Calling" wasn't just critically acclaimed; it was commercially successful, reaching audiences far beyond the punk scene. This album demonstrated that The Clash could be both punk provocateurs and mainstream musicians. It signalled a shift in the music industry, where punk, once considered a fringe movement, had become a powerful cultural force. The Clash's ability to transcend genre boundaries opened doors for punk and alternative rock bands to access a wider audience. They proved that punk could be both rebellious and commercially viable, inspiring a wave of bands to follow suit.

Their lasting impact on music, fashion, and activism remains palpable. The Clash's fearless approach to addressing pressing issues through their music and their commitment to effecting change through activism set them apart as icons of a generation. They bridged the gap between punk and mainstream rock, proving that music could be both provocative and commercially successful.

The Clash were more than a band; they were a cultural phenomenon that challenged norms, empowered the marginalized, and left an indelible mark on the world of music and beyond. Their message of rebellion, change, and unity continues to resonate, making The Clash a timeless symbol of the enduring power of music to shape the world.

**Clashes**

The Clash's journey was not without its share of internal conflicts, lineup changes, and personal struggles. While they were celebrated as one of the most influential bands in rock history, their path was marked by turbulence behind the scenes. In this section, we delve into the internal conflicts within the band, the departure of key members such as Mick Jones and Topper Headon, and The Clash's battles with substance abuse and personal issues.

While The Clash were united by a shared vision of rebellion and social consciousness, they were not immune to creative tensions within the band. The Clash's iconic songwriting duo, Joe Strummer and Mick Jones, had a dynamic that was both productive and occasionally volatile. Their differing approaches to music and songwriting often led to clashes.

Strummer, known for his passionate commitment to political activism and his desire to keep the band true to its punk roots, sometimes found himself at odds with Jones, who was more inclined toward experimentation and diversification of the band's sound.

These creative tensions were evident in the production of their 1982 album, "Combat Rock." Strummer's desire for a raw, punk sound clashed with Jones's exploration of new musical territories. The album featured tracks like "Rock the Casbah," which showcased The Clash's ability to fuse rock with reggae influences. While the album was a commercial success, it foreshadowed the growing divide within the band.

Topper Headon, the band's drummer, was a key element of The Clash's rhythm section. His drumming provided the backbone for their music. However, Headon's struggles with substance abuse became increasingly problematic. In 1982, he was dismissed from the band due to his addiction issues. Topper

Headon's battle with drug addiction was one of the most publicized aspects of The Clash's personal issues. His dismissal from the band was a painful decision but one deemed necessary for his own well-being and the band's survival.

Mick Jones, the band's lead guitarist and co-lead vocalist, was a driving force behind The Clash's music and songwriting. His departure in 1983 marked a turning point. Creative differences, amplified by tensions with Strummer, led to his exit. Jones went on to form Big Audio Dynamite, further pursuing his musical experimentation.

The departure of Jones and Headon represented a seismic shift in The Clash's lineup and creative dynamic. It signalled the end of an era, leaving a void that would be difficult to fill.

Joe Strummer, known for his passionate commitment to political activism, also grappled with personal demons. His struggles with alcohol and the pressure of being a frontman took a toll on his mental and physical health. At times, Strummer's intensity and dedication to the band's message left him emotionally drained.

Paul Simonon, the band's bassist and visual artist, had his own personal challenges to contend with. While not as prominently featured in the media for his personal struggles, the demands of touring and the band's internal tensions took their toll on him as well.

These personal issues and substance abuse problems hindered the band's creative process and strained their relationships. The Clash's chaotic lifestyle, coupled with the pressures of fame and constant touring, exacerbated these issues. Ultimately, The Clash disbanded in 1986, marking the end of an era. The band's legacy remained intact, but the internal conflicts and personal struggles had taken their toll.

Despite the challenges they faced, The Clash's legacy endures as a testament to the enduring power of their music and message. Their impact on punk and alternative rock remains profound, and their songs continue to resonate with audiences worldwide. The Clash's story is a reminder that even in the face of internal turmoil, the music they created had a transformative effect on the world of rock and roll, leaving an indelible mark on the history of music.

The Clash's breakup in 1986 marked the end of an era in rock music. The internal conflicts, lineup changes, and personal struggles that had plagued the band reached a breaking point. The departure of key members Mick Jones and Topper Headon had left a void that was difficult to fill. In an attempt to soldier on, Joe Strummer and Paul Simonon recruited new musicians and released "Cut the Crap" in 1985. However, this album was a far cry from The Clash's earlier work. It was met with mixed reviews and a lukewarm reception from both fans and critics.

"Cut the Crap" lacked the creative spark and cohesion that had defined The Clash's earlier albums. Strummer and Simonon's efforts to keep the band alive were overshadowed by the absence of Jones's songwriting and Headon's drumming. The album's sound was criticized for being overproduced, and the lyrics lacked the socio-political depth that had characterized the band's earlier work. The album marked the end of The Clash's journey as a band. They disbanded in 1986, leaving behind a legacy that would continue to evolve. The Clash's legacy is a multifaceted one that extends beyond their music. They influenced subsequent generations across various realms, including music, fashion, and activism.

The Clash's music remains as relevant today as it was during their heyday. Their songs, which addressed issues like unemployment, racial inequality, and political disenchantment, continue to resonate with audiences worldwide. Artists and activists draw ongoing inspiration from The Clash's music for its timeless messages of rebellion, unity, and change.

Songs like "London Calling," "Should I Stay or Should I Go," and "The Guns of Brixton" are anthems of defiance that still strike a chord with listeners facing contemporary social and political challenges. The Clash's willingness to speak out against injustice and their commitment to questioning the status quo serve as a blueprint for artists and activists seeking to effect change through their work.

Their music has been covered, sampled, and referenced by artists across genres, from punk to hip-hop, highlighting its enduring influence. The Clash's catalogue continues to be a source of inspiration for musicians who see music as a medium for social commentary and activism.

The Clash's place in the pantheon of rock legends is firmly secured. They are celebrated not only as pioneers of punk rock but as a band that challenged the boundaries of music, fashion, and activism. Their fearless commitment to social consciousness and rebellion elevated them to a status that transcends the punk genre. In the annals of rock history, The Clash stand as a symbol of authenticity, integrity, and unwavering commitment to their beliefs. Their music remains a touchstone for generations of fans who find solace, inspiration, and empowerment in their songs.

As rock legends, The Clash's influence and impact continue to evolve, shaping the course of music and culture for years to come. Their legacy serves as a reminder of the transformative power of music, the enduring resonance of social consciousness, and the indomitable spirit of rebellion that lives on through their timeless songs.

# LAST.TRACK.

As we draw the curtains on the chapters dedicated to The Ramones, Sex Pistols, and The Clash, we are confronted with the remarkable final act of a cultural revolution that rippled through the realms of music, fashion, and activism. The Ramones, Sex Pistols, and The Clash were not just bands; they were pioneers of a seismic shift in the world of rock and roll, and their legacies continue to resonate, challenging the status quo and inspiring generations.

**The Ramones**, with their iconic look and frenetic music, distilled punk rock to its purest essence. Leather jackets, torn jeans, and unconventional hairstyles became symbols of rebellion. Their three-chord approach was a testament to the power of simplicity and speed in music. The Ramones' minimalist style and sound laid the foundation for punk, proving that raw energy and authenticity could captivate audiences and spawn a genre that defied convention.

**The Sex Pistols**, provocateurs of punk, made their mark with "Anarchy in the UK" as a clarion call for disenchanted youth. Their rebellious attitude and confrontational lyrics shattered societal norms, creating a maelstrom of controversy. The infamous Grundy interview on British television was a snapshot of punk's audacity. The Sex Pistols' short but incandescent career ignited a punk explosion, leaving an indelible scar on the fabric of British culture and music.

**The Clash**, the genre's conscience, epitomized punk's capacity for political and social critique. Songs like "White Riot," "Clampdown," and "The Guns of Brixton" were anthems of defiance. Their commitment to addressing unemployment, racism, and inequality set them apart as activist musicians. Beyond music, they championed causes and organized benefit concerts, demonstrating that music could be a force for change.

In this final act, we are reminded that punk rock, far from fading into obscurity, endures as a state of mind, a call to action, and a source of inspiration. The Ramones, Sex Pistols, and The Clash were architects of a revolution that transcended the confines of their respective eras. Their influence on music, fashion, and activism continues to echo in the voices of artists and activists who dare to challenge, provoke, and change the world. These bands were the vanguard of a cultural movement, and their legacy serves as a testament to the enduring power of music to shape society and challenge the status quo.

# DIVISION.3

## Sonic Revolt

In the tumultuous and ever-evolving world of punk, the only constant is change. With every beat of a drum and every strum of a guitar, punk music has undergone a relentless transformation, refusing to be confined to a single sonic landscape. "Sonic Revolt" is the next chapter in our journey through the punk universe, where we plunge deeper into the heart of the genre's sonic identity.

Punk's essence is as much a sound as it is an attitude. In this section, we will peel back the layers of punk's sonic characteristics, dissecting the raw energy, simplicity, and immediacy that define this genre. We'll explore how punk became a beacon of authenticity, rejecting the polished production of mainstream music in Favor of raw, unfiltered emotion. The Ramones, with their iconic three-chord anthems, serve as our sonic guides, showing us the power of simplicity in an era of musical complexity.

As punk matured, it spawned a subgenre that pushed the boundaries of speed and aggression—hardcore punk. Born from the streets of Los Angeles and Washington, D.C., hardcore punk discarded restraint, embracing blistering guitar riffs, breakneck tempos, and unrelenting intensity. It wasn't just music; it was a visceral and confrontational experience. Bands like Black Flag and Minor Threat ignited this sonic revolution, sparking mosh pits and DIY punk scenes worldwide. We'll dive into the heart of hardcore punk, exploring its ferocity and cultural impact.

But punk's story doesn't end with speed and aggression. As we move forward, we'll encounter post-punk, a movement that challenged and expanded punk's sonic boundaries. Post-punk was a sonic playground where experimentation, artistic evolution, and lyrical depth took centre stage. Bands like Joy Division, Siouxsie and the Banshees, and Talking Heads navigated uncharted territories, blending punk with art-rock, electronic influences, and poetic lyricism. In doing so, they challenged listeners to explore the boundaries of music and culture.

In this chapter, we embark on a sonic adventure through punk's multifaceted landscape. We'll unravel the essence of punk's sound, embrace the frenetic energy of hardcore punk, and lose ourselves in the artistic liberation of post-punk. As punk's revolution continues to reverberate through generations, we're reminded that in music, as in life, change is the only constant, and punk will always be at the forefront of that evolution.

# DIVISION.3-1

## Sonic Assault

When one thinks of punk rock, the immediate sensations that come to mind are often of raw, unbridled energy and a visceral, unfiltered sound. Punk's sonic energy is its heartbeat, the driving force that propels it forward as a genre and as a cultural movement. Here, we'll delve deep into the essence of punk's sonic characteristics, understanding how its music and attitude converge to create a one-of-a-kind sonic experience. We'll also dissect the deliberate rejection of polished production values in Favor of raw authenticity, a choice that would come to define the very soul of punk.

At its core, punk music is an adrenaline-fueled whirlwind. It's a sound that slams into your eardrums with the force of a sledgehammer, leaving you exhilarated and, at times, breathless. This visceral and unfiltered nature of punk's sonic energy is what sets it apart from other genres. The instruments, often played with furious intensity, seem like extensions of the musicians' very beings, a conduit for their pent-up frustrations, hopes, and fears.

Punk's energy is immediate, unapologetic, and spontaneous. It doesn't wait for perfection; it thrives on imperfection. This urgency translates into blistering guitar riffs, pounding drums, and vocals that range from defiant shouts to raw, emotional cries. Bands like The Ramones, The Sex Pistols, and The Clash harnessed this energy, turning it into a cathartic experience for themselves and their audiences.

What truly distinguishes punk from other genres is the symbiotic relationship between its music and attitude. Punk is not just about the notes played or the words sung; it's about the ethos that underpins every chord and lyric. The music and attitude are inseparable, feeding off each other to create an authentic sonic experience.

Punk's attitude is one of rebellion, a rejection of the status quo and a challenge to the establishment. This attitude permeates the music, infusing it with a sense of defiance and purpose. Whether it's The Ramones' call for a "Rockaway Beach" getaway or The Sex Pistols' declaration of "Anarchy in the UK," punk's sonic energy serves as the sonic battleground for this rebellion.

In punk, authenticity is paramount. Musicians don't hide behind layers of studio production; they expose themselves, flaws and all, in their music. This authenticity is reflected not only in the lyrics but also in the raw, unadulterated sound that emanates from their instruments. Punk's energy is a testament to the sincerity and unapologetic honesty of its creators.

One of the most defining aspects of punk's sonic energy is its deliberate rejection of polished production values. Unlike the meticulously crafted albums of mainstream music, punk recordings often have a rough, DIY quality. This is not a flaw but a conscious choice made to preserve the authenticity and immediacy of the music.

In the early days of punk, many bands recorded their songs quickly and inexpensively, often in small, independent studios or even live settings. This approach allowed them to capture the raw essence of their music without the gloss and overproduction that characterized mainstream rock. The imperfections in the recordings became badges of Honor, testaments to the unfiltered nature of punk.

Furthermore, the rejection of polished production extended to live performances. Punk bands thrived in small, sweaty clubs where the energy was palpable, and the barrier between performer and audience was practically non-existent. The spontaneity and imperfection of these live shows added to the overall rawness and authenticity of the punk experience.

In peeling back, the layers of punk's sonic identity, we reveal its visceral, unfiltered nature, its symbiotic relationship between music and attitude, and its deliberate rejection of polished production values in Favor of raw authenticity. Punk's sonic energy is not merely a backdrop to its rebellion; it is the sonic manifestation of that rebellion.

Punk's rawness and immediacy resonate with audiences because they speak to the core of human emotion. The imperfections, the unbridled passion, and the authenticity all combine to create a unique sonic experience that is as powerful today as it was when punk first emerged. In punk, we find not just music but a statement, a call to arms, and a reminder that sometimes, the most potent form of rebellion is the unfiltered, unapologetic sound of a distorted guitar and a voice raised in defiance.

In the realm of music, complexity often reigns supreme. Orchestral arrangements, intricate harmonies, and virtuosic performances have long been celebrated as the pinnacle of musical achievement. However, within this intricate tapestry of sound, there emerged a genre that dared to challenge the status quo—a genre that revelled in its simplicity, its unadorned authenticity, and its raw emotional power. This genre is none other than punk rock.

At its core, punk music is a testament to the beauty of simplicity. Unlike the elaborate compositions of classical music or the intricate layers of progressive rock, punk revels in its minimalist approach. This minimalism extends to various aspects of punk's musical structure, starting with its basic chord progressions. Punk compositions are often built on three or four simple chords, eschewing the need for intricate harmonies or complex melodies.

The stripped-down nature of punk is not limited to its harmonic structure; it extends to its rhythmic elements as well. Drum patterns in punk songs are typically straightforward, with a focus on maintaining a steady, driving beat. Basslines, too, are often uncomplicated, providing a solid foundation for the rest of the band to build upon.

Punk's minimalistic approach is not confined solely to the composition of songs but also extends to their arrangements. In stark contrast to the lush orchestrations of orchestral music or the multi-layered production of mainstream rock, punk songs often feature a "less is more" philosophy. Guitar solos, if they exist at all, are short and to the point. There is no room for musical extravagance in punk.

This minimalist approach extends to the duration of punk songs as well. Unlike the extended jams of some rock genres, punk tracks are typically concise, with many clocking in at two minutes or less. This brevity is not a result of limitation but a conscious choice to deliver a powerful, concentrated burst of music. In punk, every second counts, and there is no room for filler.

One might wonder why punk, a genre celebrated for its simplicity, has had such a profound impact on the world of music. The answer lies in the power of simplicity as an emotive tool. By paring down their music to its bare essentials, punk bands create a raw and unfiltered sonic experience that speaks directly to the listener's emotions.

In punk, simplicity becomes a means of emphasizing emotion and immediacy. The straightforward chord progressions and uncomplicated melodies allow for an unobstructed connection between the musician and the listener. There are no intricate layers to dissect; there is only the unvarnished truth of the music.

Furthermore, the brevity of punk songs contributes to this sense of immediacy. With no time to meander or indulge in extended instrumental passages, punk bands cut to the chase. The lyrics and melodies hit hard and fast, leaving a lasting impact in a matter of minutes. This immediacy is a hallmark of punk's emotional resonance.

In the world of music, punk stands as a defiant reminder that complexity is not the sole measure of musical merit. Instead, punk celebrates the beauty of simplicity, using minimalistic arrangements and straightforward compositions to convey raw emotion and immediacy. This simplicity is not a limitation but a choice—a choice to reject the excesses of musical extravagance in Favor of unadulterated authenticity. In the raw, unfiltered sound of a punk song, we find not only simplicity but also honesty, rebellion, and a refusal to conform to conventional musical norms. Punk's simplicity is a sonic rebellion in itself, a reminder that sometimes, the most potent messages are delivered with the fewest notes and the most fervent spirit.

# DIVISION.3-2

## Assault Method

Punk rock, with its raw energy and rebellious spirit, had already made a significant impact on the music scene by the late 1970s. However, as the genre continued to evolve, it spawned a subgenre that would push the boundaries of speed, aggression, and intensity—hardcore punk. In this exploration, we'll journey back to the historical context and geographical origins of this subgenre, dissect the factors that led to its emergence as a distinct musical force, and delve into the early bands and scenes that played pivotal roles in its development.

To understand the birth of hardcore punk, it's essential to consider the historical context in which it emerged. The late 1970s were marked by social and political turbulence in the United States. Economic struggles, urban decay, and disillusionment with mainstream culture fuelled a sense of frustration and alienation among many young people. This discontent found its voice in punk rock, a genre that rejected the excesses of the music industry and called for a return to authenticity and simplicity.

Geographically, two cities played central roles in the birth of hardcore punk: Los Angeles and Washington, D.C. While both cities contributed to the subgenre's development, they each had their unique characteristics and scenes. Several factors converged to give rise to hardcore punk. First and foremost was the desire for a more aggressive and uncompromising sound. Many early punk bands, such as The Ramones and The Sex Pistols, had already paved the way with their fast tempos and stripped-down approach. However, for some musicians and fans, this wasn't extreme enough. There was a hunger for something faster, louder, and more unrelenting.

Another crucial factor was the DIY (Do It Yourself) ethos that had become synonymous with punk culture. Hardcore punk embraced this ethos wholeheartedly. Bands started booking their own shows, releasing their own records, and creating their own zines and promotional materials. This newfound self-reliance allowed hardcore punk to flourish outside the mainstream music industry, maintaining its independence and authenticity.

The punk scene had also grown larger and more diverse. As punk gained popularity, it attracted a wide range of individuals who brought their own perspectives and influences to the genre. This diversity helped spawn subgenres like hardcore punk, as musicians incorporated elements from other genres like metal, skateboarding culture, and even elements of political activism.

In Los Angeles, bands like Black Flag, The Germs, and X emerged as pioneers, as pointed out by MasterClass (2021). The city's punk scene had already gained a reputation for its intensity, but these bands took it to a new level. Black Flag, led by the enigmatic Henry Rollins, became known for their blistering live shows and uncompromising attitude. The Germs, with their chaotic performances, embodied the wild and unpredictable nature of hardcore.

In Washington, D.C., a thriving punk scene known for its political activism and DIY ethos began to take shape. Bands like Minor Threat, Bad Brains, and Teen Idles became icons of D.C. hardcore. Minor Threat, in particular, would leave an indelible mark on the genre with their "straight edge" philosophy, which promoted sobriety and self-discipline—a stark contrast to the excesses often associated with rock and roll.

These early bands and scenes were instrumental in shaping the hardcore punk sound and ethos. They provided a template for future generations of hardcore musicians and fans, setting the stage for a subculture that would continue to evolve and diversify.

The birth of hardcore punk represents a pivotal moment in the evolution of punk rock. Fuelled by dissatisfaction with the status quo, a hunger for speed and aggression, and a commitment to DIY principles, hardcore punk emerged as a distinct subgenre with its own unique identity. Los Angeles and

Washington, D.C., served as its birthplaces, each contributing to the subgenre's development in its own way. It would go on to influence countless bands and scenes worldwide, leaving an indelible mark on the landscape of punk rock and continuing to serve as a source of inspiration for those who seek a musical outlet for their frustrations and passions. It was, and remains, a sonic revolution.

### Assault Weapons

In the world of music, few genres can match the sheer ferocity and unrelenting intensity of hardcore punk. Hardcore punk's sonic elements combine to create a visceral and confrontational listening experience like no other. In this exploration of "Assault Weapons," we will dissect the very anatomy of hardcore punk, analysing blistering guitar riffs, breakneck tempos, and aggressive vocal delivery. We will discuss how these characteristics serve as the driving force behind the genre, conveying its message and ethos with unparalleled intensity.

At the core of hardcore punk's sonic assault are its blistering guitar riffs. These are not the leisurely, melodic lines found in other genres; they are lightning-fast, frenetic, and unapologetically aggressive. The power of hardcore punk guitar riffs lies not in complexity but in their unrelenting attack.

The simplicity of hardcore guitar riffs allows for maximum impact. Bands often utilize power chords, palm muting, and relentless downstrokes to create a wall of sound that pummels the listener into submission. The guitar becomes an assault weapon, a sonic sledgehammer that drives the music forward with unwavering force.

What sets hardcore punk guitar riffs apart is their sheer speed. They are played at a breakneck tempo that leaves little room for respite. This rapid-fire approach, often described as "chugging," propels the music with a relentless momentum that matches the urgency of the genre's lyrical themes. If the guitar riffs are the heartbeat of hardcore punk, then the breakneck tempos are its lifeblood. Hardcore is, by nature, a fast-paced genre, and it thrives on this sense of urgency. Songs often race from start to finish, leaving listeners exhilarated and breathless.

The tempo of hardcore punk is a critical element in creating a visceral and confrontational listening experience. It reflects the genre's confrontational attitude and its rejection of complacency. When a hardcore punk song begins, there is no gentle introduction; it launches forward with full force, demanding the listener's attention. This rapid tempo serves multiple purposes. It creates a sense of urgency and immediacy, aligning with the lyrical themes of frustration, discontent, and rebellion. It also fuels the energy of live performances, where the intensity of the music is mirrored by the physicality of the mosh pit and the fervour of the crowd.

While blistering guitar riffs and breakneck tempos define the sonic landscape of hardcore punk, it is the aggressive vocal delivery that serves as the genre's voice. Hardcore vocalists are not here to serenade; they are here to confront, challenge, and provoke.

The vocal style in hardcore punk is characterized by its raw intensity. Vocalists often employ harsh, shouted, and sometimes even screamed vocals. These are not polished melodies but impassioned declarations. The lyrics are delivered with a sense of urgency, as if the vocalist is directly addressing the listener with a call to action.

The aggression in the vocal delivery is a reflection of the genre's confrontational ethos. Hardcore punk lyrics frequently address social issues, political dissent, and personal struggles. The aggressive vocal style becomes a vehicle for expressing these themes with unfiltered emotion. It is a form of catharsis, a way to vent frustrations and convey a message that demands to be heard.

At the heart of hardcore punk's assault weapon sound lies the concept of intensity. It is this intensity that defines the genre, conveying its message and ethos with unyielding force. The blistering guitar riffs, breakneck tempos, and aggressive vocal delivery are not mere stylistic choices; they are the tools through which hardcore punk communicates its rebellion, its dissent, and its passion.

Hardcore punk's intensity serves as a sonic blitzkrieg, a full-frontal assault on the senses. It is an experience that demands engagement and provokes a visceral response. Whether through the relentless guitar riffs, the breakneck tempos, or the confrontational vocals, hardcore punk confronts complacency and challenges the status quo.

In conclusion, "Assault Weapons" in hardcore punk represent the genre's unapologetic commitment to intensity and confrontation. Blistering guitar riffs, breakneck tempos, and aggressive vocal delivery are the sonic elements that define this subgenre, creating a visceral and confrontational listening experience. In the world of hardcore punk, intensity is not a byproduct; it is the very essence of the music—a relentless assault on the senses that demands attention and refuses to be ignored.

Battle Scars

Hardcore punk, with its blistering sound and confrontational attitude, was more than just a subgenre of music. It was a cultural force that left indelible "Battle Scars" on the social and musical landscape, both locally and globally. In this exploration, we will delve into the cultural impact of hardcore punk, examining its roots, its formation of mosh pits, and the DIY ethos that defined the scene. We will also uncover the lasting influence of pioneering bands like Black Flag and Minor Threat, whose music and ethos continue to resonate with subsequent generations of punk and alternative music.

Hardcore punk emerged in the late 1970s and early 1980s. It was a genre characterized by its intensity, speed, and rawness, and it carried with it a confrontational attitude that challenged the status quo.

Locally, hardcore punk scenes began to take root in cities across the United States, with Los Angeles, Washington, D.C., and New York City serving as key epicentres. These scenes were fuelled by a sense of discontent and a desire for something more immediate and aggressive than what mainstream music had to offer. Hardcore punk became a rallying point for disenfranchised youth who sought an outlet for their frustrations.

Globally, hardcore punk found resonance among like-minded individuals who identified with its rebellious spirit. It spread to countries far beyond its

American birthplace, influencing scenes in Europe, Asia, and beyond. This global reach demonstrated the universality of the genre's message and ethos.

One of the most iconic and enduring aspects of hardcore punk culture is the formation of mosh pits during live performances. Moshing is a physical expression of the intensity that defines the genre. It involves audience members engaging in aggressive, often frenetic dancing in a designated area near the stage.

Mosh pits serve as a release valve for the pent-up energy of hardcore punk's music and lyrics. They are a communal experience where individuals come together to share in the intensity of the music. Moshing is not an act of violence but a form of catharsis, a way for fans to connect with the music and with each other.

The chaotic nature of mosh pits reflects the confrontational ethos of hardcore punk. It is a space where participants can push boundaries, both physical and emotional, in a controlled and communal setting. While it may appear aggressive to outsiders, moshing is an integral part of the hardcore punk experience, and it has persisted as a defining feature of the genre's live performances.

Central to the hardcore punk scene was the DIY ethos, a philosophy that emphasized self-reliance, independence, and grassroots organizing. In contrast to the mainstream music industry, which often seemed distant and inaccessible, hardcore punk bands and fans embraced the idea of doing it themselves.

This DIY ethos manifested in various ways. Bands recorded their own music, produced their own records, and booked their own shows. Fanzines, or homemade magazines, were created to share information, interviews, and reviews within the scene. DIY record labels, such as Dischord Records in Washington, D.C., and SST Records in Los Angeles, were founded to support and distribute hardcore punk music.

The DIY ethos empowered individuals to take control of their own creative and musical destinies. It fostered a sense of ownership and independence that resonated deeply with those within the hardcore punk scene. This spirit of self-reliance not only helped the scene flourish but also inspired countless individuals to pursue their creative passions outside the confines of mainstream conventions.

Pioneering bands like Black Flag and Minor Threat played instrumental roles in shaping the sound and ethos of hardcore punk. Their influence extended far beyond their respective scenes and eras, leaving an indelible mark on subsequent generations of punk and alternative music.

**Black Flag**, with its relentless touring and uncompromising attitude, set a precedent for DIY ethics and an unrelenting work ethic. The band's music, characterized by its aggressive guitar riffs and the distinctive vocal delivery of Henry Rollins, continues to inspire punk and alternative bands seeking authenticity and intensity.

**Minor Threat**, led by Ian MacKaye, introduced the "straight edge" philosophy, promoting sobriety and self-discipline. This ethos became a significant aspect of hardcore punk culture and remains a defining feature for those who identify as straight edge.

The influence of these bands can be heard in the music of subsequent generations of punk and alternative artists. Hardcore punk's intensity, DIY ethos, and confrontational attitude continue to shape the sonic and cultural landscape, inspiring new waves of musicians to challenge the status quo and convey their messages with unwavering authenticity.

The cultural impact of hardcore punk, as explored through its formation of mosh pits, DIY ethos, and the enduring influence of pioneering bands, is a testament to the genre's enduring legacy. It left "Battle Scars" on the musical and social landscape, both locally and globally. Hardcore punk empowered a generation to confront the status quo, express themselves authentically, and create a community that valued intensity and independence above all else.

The scene's resilience and longevity are a testament to its enduring appeal. Hardcore punk, with its raw energy and unapologetic attitude, continues to resonate with those who seek a musical outlet for their frustrations and a culture that values authenticity and intensity above all else. It is a legacy that lives on, leaving its mark on the battle-scarred terrain of music and culture.

# DIVISION.3-3

## Post-Punk

In the annals of music history, evolution is the heartbeat of any genre. As punk's raw intensity continued to resonate in the late 1970s and early 1980s, it spawned a new movement—one that would push the boundaries of sound, challenge conventions, and redefine the sonic landscape. Within these pages, we will explore the historical context that gave rise to post-punk, dissect its unique sonic characteristics and experimentation, and unravel the lyrical depth that set it apart. Welcome to the artistic evolution of post-punk.

To understand post-punk, we must first understand the historical context that birthed this creative and boundary-pushing movement. The late 1970s were a time of tumultuous change, both culturally and politically. Punk, as a genre, had already made its mark, but its simplicity and rawness left room for exploration. It was against this backdrop that post-punk emerged, challenging the established norms and expanding the possibilities of punk's rebellious ethos.

This section will journey through the historical context that led to the emergence of post-punk as a distinct movement. We will explore the societal shifts, musical influences, and cultural currents that fuelled its inception. Along the way, we will shine a spotlight on the key bands and artists who played pivotal roles in shaping the post-punk landscape.

At its core, post-punk is a testament to the power of artistic evolution and sonic exploration. It is a movement that pushed the boundaries of what punk could be, infusing it with a wide array of influences and unconventional instrumentation. We will delve into the sonic elements and characteristics that define post-punk, including its fusion of punk with art-rock, electronic influences, and experimental soundscapes.

Post-punk was a playground where experimentation took centre stage. Bands sought to defy expectations, embracing a diverse range of musical influences. We will discuss how experimentation and artistic evolution became central to post-punk's sound and how bands approached songwriting, composition, and arrangements in unique and innovative ways.

What sets post-punk apart from its punk predecessors is not only its sonic innovation but also its lyrical depth and impact. We will explore the lyrical themes and poetic lyricism that became hallmarks of the genre. Post-punk bands ventured into uncharted territory, addressing social and existential themes with eloquence and depth.

We will delve into the ways post-punk bands tackled issues that went beyond the surface, crafting lyrics that were thought-provoking and introspective. Additionally, we will examine the cultural and musical impact of post-punk, including its influence on subsequent genres and artists who drew inspiration from its unique blend of sonic experimentation and lyrical depth.

Join us in the exploration of post-punk, a movement that not only challenged the boundaries of sound but also left an enduring mark on the landscape of music and culture. It is a chapter in the story of sonic revolution that continues to resonate with artists and audiences alike, reminding us of the ever-evolving nature of artistic expression.

### The Emergence of Post-Punk

In the ever-evolving tapestry of musical history, the emergence of post-punk stands as a testament to the relentless drive of artists to push boundaries, challenge conventions, and redefine sonic landscapes. We will delve into the social, cultural, and musical currents that converged to create post-punk, explore how it both challenged and expanded upon the sonic boundaries set by punk, and illuminate the key bands and artists who played pivotal roles in shaping this remarkable chapter in music history.

To grasp the emergence of post-punk, we must peel back the layers of historical context that set the stage for this genre-defying movement. The late 1970s were a time of profound social and cultural change, a period marked by turbulence and transition. The initial wave of punk had already stormed the musical scene, leaving its mark with a raw, rebellious energy that captivated youth around the world. But as the decade progressed, the punk ethos of simplicity and immediacy left room for exploration.

One of the defining characteristics of this era was a sense of disillusionment, particularly among young people. Economic challenges, political unrest, and a prevailing sense of disconnection from mainstream culture fuelled a desire for more depth and complexity in music. Punk had torn down the barriers between artist and audience, democratizing music production and performance. Yet, in its wake, a new hunger for artistic evolution and experimentation arose.

Post-punk emerged as a response to this hunger, serving as a radical departure from the sonic boundaries set by punk. While punk had thrived on its simplicity and straightforward aggression, post-punk dared to challenge these established norms. It was a movement that expanded the possibilities of what punk could be, opening doors to a myriad of influences and musical exploration.

At its core, post-punk retained punk's rebellious ethos but introduced a sonic complexity that was both innovative and challenging. Bands began to fuse punk with elements of art-rock, electronic influences, and unconventional instrumentation. This fusion allowed for a new level of sonic experimentation and artistic evolution, breaking away from the limitations of three-chord anthems and embracing a more diverse range of musical possibilities.

The sonic landscape of post-punk was marked by atmospheric textures, intricate arrangements, and a willingness to embrace unconventional sounds. This departure from punk's sonic simplicity was a testament to the genre's commitment to artistic growth and sonic exploration.

As post-punk began to take shape, key bands and artists emerged as pioneers, shaping the sonic and cultural landscape of the movement. These visionaries played pivotal roles in defining post-punk's sound and ethos, leaving an indelible mark on the genre and its evolution.

One of the most influential bands of this era was Joy Division. Hailing from Manchester, England, Joy Division's brooding, atmospheric sound and introspective lyrics epitomized the post-punk aesthetic. Ian Curtis, the band's enigmatic frontman, captivated audiences with his haunting vocals and emotionally charged lyrics. Songs like "Love Will Tear Us Apart" and "Transmission" became anthems of a generation, blending the intensity of punk with an atmospheric and melancholic depth.

Another cornerstone of the post-punk movement was Siouxsie and the Banshees. Led by the captivating Siouxsie Sioux, the band defied categorization with their eclectic sound, blending punk aggression with elements of art-rock and gothic aesthetics. Their album "Juju" remains a seminal work in the post-punk canon, showcasing a sonic palette that transcended genre boundaries.

As we navigate the emergence of post-punk, it becomes evident that these pioneering voices were instrumental in shaping the genre's trajectory. Their willingness to challenge conventions, embrace experimentation, and delve into complex lyrical themes paved the way for a movement that would leave an indelible mark on the world of music.

The emergence of post-punk represents a critical chapter in the evolution of music—a movement born from the hunger for artistic evolution and a desire to transcend the boundaries of sound. It was a response to a changing world, a cultural landscape in flux, and a generation seeking depth and complexity in music.

In this journey through history, we have uncovered the historical context that gave rise to post-punk, explored how it challenged and expanded upon the sonic boundaries set by punk, and highlighted the key bands and artists who carved their names into the genre's annals. Post-punk would go on to become a sonic revolution, pushing music into uncharted territories, and leaving an enduring legacy that continues to inspire artists and audiences alike.

**Sonic Exploration in Post-Punk**

In the realm of music, evolution is the heartbeat of creativity. Post-punk, emerging in the late 1970s and flourishing throughout the 1980s, was a testament to this concept. It challenged the established norms and sonic boundaries set by punk, embarking on a journey of unparalleled exploration. Let's discuss how experimentation and artistic evolution became central to post-punk's sound, and we will examine how post-punk bands approached songwriting, composition, and arrangements in ways that pushed the boundaries of musical convention.

One of the defining features of post-punk is its fusion of punk with art-rock sensibilities. This amalgamation birthed a sonic palette of complexity and sophistication, diverging from the straightforward aggression of punk. Post-punk bands drew inspiration from the art-rock movement of the 1970s, which valued experimentation, unconventional song structures, and a focus on artistic expression.

This fusion introduced a multifaceted approach to post-punk's sonic landscape. Bands began to incorporate elements such as intricate guitar work, atmospheric textures, and a willingness to embrace a broader range of influences. Whereas punk had often thrived on simplicity, post-punk aimed for intricacy, layering sounds and melodies to create a rich and immersive sonic experience.

The sonic exploration within post-punk was not merely about pushing boundaries for the sake of it; it was about conveying a deeper emotional and artistic depth. Bands like Gang of Four and Public Image Ltd. (PiL) embraced this fusion, infusing their music with thought-provoking lyricism and innovative soundscapes.

Another dimension of post-punk's sonic exploration was its embrace of electronic influences. This departure from traditional rock instrumentation marked a significant shift in the genre's sonic landscape. Bands began to incorporate synthesizers, drum machines, and electronic effects, expanding their sonic toolkit.

The integration of electronic elements allowed post-punk to pioneer what would become the future sound of music. Bands like Depeche Mode and New

Order ventured into the realm of electronic music, marrying it with post-punk's introspective lyricism. The result was a fusion that not only challenged the boundaries of rock but also laid the foundation for the electronic and synth-pop movements of the 1980s.

Experimentation with electronic elements in post-punk was not confined to studio experimentation; it extended to live performances as well. Bands like The Cure incorporated synthesizers and drum machines into their stage setups, pushing the boundaries of what was possible in a live setting and foreshadowing the electronic revolution that would follow.

Post-punk also dared to redefine the sound through unconventional instrumentation. Traditional rock instruments were not the sole focus; instead, artists sought to expand their sonic horizons by incorporating a diverse array of instruments and sounds. This willingness to embrace unconventional instrumentation led to the inclusion of instruments like saxophones, violins, and even brass sections in post-punk compositions. Bands like The Birthday Party and The Swans explored dissonance and unconventional song structures, crafting music that was as challenging as it was captivating.

The approach to percussion was similarly innovative. Drummers experimented with polyrhythms, unconventional time signatures, and intricate patterns that pushed the boundaries of rhythm and added layers of complexity to post-punk compositions.

Central to post-punk's sonic exploration was a unique approach to songwriting, composition, and arrangements. Bands sought to challenge the conventions of musical structure, creating songs that defied easy categorization. One hallmark of post-punk songwriting was its departure from verse-chorus-verse structures. Instead, songs often unfolded in a more fluid and narrative fashion, allowing for a greater sense of storytelling and emotional depth. This approach emphasized lyrics and their role in conveying complex themes and emotions.

Composition and arrangements were equally unconventional. Bands embraced dissonance, asymmetry, and irregular song lengths, shattering the traditional melds of pop and rock. This departure from convention allowed post-punk artists to craft music that was both intellectually stimulating and emotionally resonant.

Post-punk dared to fuse punk with art-rock, embrace electronic influences, and explore unconventional instrumentation, reshaping the sonic landscape for generations to come. It was a movement that challenged the norms of songwriting, composition, and arrangements, crafting music that defied easy categorization and invited listeners on a journey of sonic discovery. Post-punk's legacy is one of artistic evolution and a relentless pursuit of new sonic frontiers, leaving an indelible mark on the world of music.

### Post-Punk's Lyrical Depth and Impact

In the realm of music, lyrics are the poetic soul that breathes life into a song. Post-punk, emerging as a distinct movement in the late 1970s and flourishing throughout the 1980s, distinguished itself not only through its sonic experimentation but also through the profound lyrical depth and impact it brought to the forefront. Here we will discuss how post-punk bands addressed a range of themes, from the social to the existential, in their lyrics, and we will examine the cultural and musical impact of post-punk, including its enduring influence on subsequent genres and artists.

Post-punk emerged as a response to the simplicity and immediacy of punk, and its lyrical approach was no exception. While punk had often embraced straightforward and confrontational lyricism, post-punk bands sought to infuse their songs with poetic depth and intellectual complexity.

One of the defining characteristics of post-punk's lyrical approach was its introspective exploration of themes. Bands delved into the human condition, relationships, alienation, and existentialism with a depth that went beyond the surface. This depth often manifested in abstract and metaphorical lyricism, inviting listeners to engage with the material on multiple levels.

Joy Division, with Ian Curtis as its enigmatic lyricist, epitomized this lyrical depth. Songs like "Love Will Tear Us Apart" and "Atmosphere" explored themes of love, isolation, and mortality with an emotional rawness that struck a chord with audiences. Curtis's poetic lyricism invited listeners to contemplate the profound and often melancholic aspects of the human experience.

Siouxsie and the Banshees, led by Siouxsie Sioux, also embraced poetic lyricism. Their song "Spellbound" is a prime example, with lyrics that merge vivid imagery and cryptic symbolism. Siouxsie's lyrical approach created an air of mystery and intrigue that drew listeners into a world of artistic exploration.

Post-punk's lyrical canvas was not limited to introspection; it also extended to the exploration of social and existential themes. Bands sought to confront the issues of their time, providing commentary on the cultural and societal landscapes in which they lived.

Many post-punk bands used their music as a platform to address social and political issues. Gang of Four, for instance, infused their songs with biting social commentary, critiquing consumerism, capitalism, and power structures. Their track "At Home He's a Tourist" dissected the tension between individual desires and societal pressures.

The Clash, while often associated with punk, also delved into post-punk territory with songs like "London Calling." This iconic track served as both a rallying cry and a commentary on the state of London and the world at the time. Its lyrics addressed issues of impending catastrophe, cultural decay, and social unrest, mirroring the turbulent times in which it was written.

Existential themes also found their place in post-punk lyrics. Bands like The Smiths, known for their introspective and melancholic songs, explored the human experience through themes of isolation, longing, and identity. Morrissey's lyrical prowess elevated The Smiths to iconic status, with songs like "How Soon Is Now?" resonating with listeners on a deeply personal level.

The cultural and musical impact of post-punk cannot be overstated. Beyond its sonic experimentation, post-punk's lyrical depth and thematic exploration helped shape the musical and cultural landscape of the late 20th century and beyond.

Post-punk's influence extended into the realms of goth, new wave, and alternative rock, leaving an indelible mark on subsequent genres and artists. Bands like R.E.M., The Cure, and Radiohead drew inspiration from post-punk's lyrical complexity and thematic depth, crafting music that challenged listeners both emotionally and intellectually.

Culturally, post-punk contributed to a broader shift in the role of lyrics in popular music. It demonstrated that music could serve as a vehicle for thought-provoking commentary and artistic expression. This legacy is evident in the continued exploration of lyrical depth by subsequent generations of musicians in various genres.

# LAST.TRACK.

In the grand symphony of music's evolution, the "Sonic Revolt" chapter serves as a compelling crescendo—a harmonious exploration of the diverse facets of sound, creativity, and cultural impact. From the raw simplicity of punk to the unbridled intensity of hardcore punk and the artistic evolution of post-punk, this chapter has journeyed through sonic landscapes that challenged the status quo and redefined the boundaries of musical expression. As we reflect on the multifaceted tapestry of this chapter, we encounter a story of artistic rebellion, innovation, and enduring influence.

Our voyage began with the essence of punk—a sound as much an attitude as a musical genre. The simplicity, immediacy, and rejection of polished production values became the sonic hallmarks of punk. Bands like The Ramones epitomized this ethos, wielding three chords like a musical sledgehammer. The Ramones taught us that music need not be complex to be impactful, and their legacy continues to inspire artists seeking authenticity in an era of musical complexity.

Our journey then shifted to the ferocious heart of hardcore punk—a subgenre born from the streets and fuelled by blistering riffs and unrelenting intensity. Bands like Black Flag and Minor Threat became the heralds of a confrontational experience, sparking mosh pits and DIY punk scenes worldwide. Hardcore punk's impact transcended sound; it fostered a culture of rebellion and activism, nurturing the punk spirit for generations.

Finally, we explored post-punk—an era that challenged and expanded upon the sonic boundaries set by punk. Post-punk was a movement that embraced complexity, poetic lyricism, and thematic depth. Bands like Joy Division and Siouxsie and the Banshees elevated the art of lyrical storytelling, exploring themes that ranged from love and isolation to social commentary. Post-punk's legacy continues to reverberate through the musical and lyrical explorations of subsequent generations of artists.

As we conclude this chapter, we are left with a resounding truth: music is an ever-evolving art form, capable of transcending cultural and temporal boundaries. The sonic revolutions we've explored have left an indelible mark on music's history, shaping the way we perceive and create sound. They remind us that authenticity, intensity, and complexity are not mutually exclusive but rather facets of a dynamic creative continuum.

This chapter has unveiled the essence of sonic revolution—a relentless drive to challenge conventions, to innovate, and to express the human experience through the language of sound. It serves as a testament to the power of music to reflect and shape the world around us. The echoes of punk's simplicity, hardcore punk's ferocity, and post-punk's artistic depth continue to resound in the music we cherish today, guiding us toward new frontiers of sonic exploration. As we turn the page, we carry with us the echoes of these revolutions, eager to discover the next chapter in music's ever-evolving journey.

# DIVISION.4

## Activism, Politics, & Society

The world of punk rock has never been just about music. From its inception, it has been an arena where activism, politics, and society intertwine with the unapologetic and rebellious sounds that define the genre. As we delve into this multifaceted realm, we explore the powerful forces of anarchy, activism, and rebellion that have been pivotal in shaping punk's identity.

At the heart of punk's ethos lies a fundamental rejection of authority, a celebration of individualism, and an unyielding desire to challenge societal norms. This chapter opens with an exploration of anarchy and activism within punk. We unearth the historical roots of this rebellious spirit, tracing it back to countercultural movements that birthed the seeds of anarchy in punk's sonic landscape. From the Beat Generation of the 1950s, with figures like Jack Kerouac and Allen Ginsberg, to the socio-political upheaval of the 1960s, we illuminate how these influences gave rise to punk's revolutionary energy.

We take a deep dive into the subversive world of anarcho-punk and the associated crust punk movements. These subgenres embraced radical activism, promoting ideals of sobriety, DIY ethics, and uncompromising integrity. Bands like Crass and Discharge are our guides as we navigate through the intense, chaotic, and politically charged landscape of anarcho-punk. Their music served as a call to arms, challenging the establishment and advocating for socio-political change. This section unveils how anarchy, in its most visceral form, has manifested within punk, leaving an indelible mark on its history.

We delve into the diverse and inclusive facets of punk. It highlights how punk has provided a platform for marginalized voices, addressing issues of sexuality, gender, and feminism. The LGBTQ+ community found solace and expression within punk's unfiltered authenticity. Bands like Pansy Division and Bikini Kill broke barriers, addressing LGBTQ+ experiences and feminist ideals head-on. Through their music, they challenged conventional gender norms and advocated for equality. This chapter celebrates the rich tapestry of punk that transcends societal boundaries, making it a driving force for social change.

Throughout this exploration of anarchy, activism, and the many facets of punk's social and political engagement, we will uncover the ways in which punk's rebellious spirit has ignited social movements, challenged norms, and given voice to the marginalized. Punk has always been more than just music; it is a catalyst for dissent, a vessel for social critique, and a mirror reflecting the ever-evolving landscape of activism and politics. Join us as we embark on a journey through the heart of punk's activist soul, where music and societal change collide in a harmonious cacophony.

# DIVISION.4-1

### Anarchy, Activism, & Punk

The rebellious spirit of punk finds its roots in the Beat Generation of the 1950s and the countercultural upheaval of the 1960s. Figures like Jack Kerouac, Allen Ginsberg, and William S. Burroughs rejected societal norms, championing individualism and questioning conventions, setting the stage for punk's ethos. Musicians such as Bob Dylan and bands like The Doors used music for social critique during the 1960s, challenging conventional boundaries. This subversive energy culminated in the punk movement of the 1970s, characterized by a rejection of authority and an embrace of nonconformity, influencing punk's music, fashion, and attitude.

At the heart of punk's subversive energy lies a visceral rejection of societal norms, a vehement defiance that finds its roots in the stifling conservatism and complacency of the 1970s. This decade was marked by economic instability and political disillusionment, and it was within this turbulent context that punk emerged as a direct response, challenging the status quo with a fervour that would come to define a generation. Bands like The Ramones, The Sex Pistols, and The Clash served as sonic revolutionaries, channelling the frustration and disillusionment of disaffected youth into music that became a rallying cry for change.

Punk celebrated nonconformity and individualism. It emphasized accessible music creation, prioritizing raw expression and passion over complexity. This commitment extended to diverse subgenres: Hardcore punk, like Black Flag and Minor Threat, amped up aggression with blistering riffs, breakneck tempos, and fierce vocals, challenging the need for technical intricacies. Post-punk, seen in Joy Division and Talking Heads, pushed punk's boundaries, blending art-rock, electronics, and unconventional instruments, highlighting its adaptability and innovation. In all its forms, punk provided a versatile platform for nonconformity and individualism.

Punk's subversive spirit extends to fashion, where individuality takes centre stage. Leather jackets adorned with patches and pins, torn jeans, and unconventional hairstyles defy mainstream aesthetics. Punk fashion celebrates nonconformity and self-expression, providing a platform for those who reject societal norms. It communicates dissent and individuality, challenging the homogenized beauty ideals promoted by mainstream culture, offering a space for unique identities to shine through personal style.

Punk serves as more than a musical genre and fashion statement; it also functions as a platform for countercultural movements. Peeling back the punk activism of the 1970s to contemporary punk bands that champion social and political causes, we uncover how punk has served as a catalyst for social critique and activism.

Bands like Dead Kennedys, with their satirical lyrics and politically charged performances, used their music as a means of addressing societal issues and motivating change. The punk spirit of resistance continues in contemporary punk bands, who champion causes like environmentalism and social justice, raising awareness and funds through benefit shows and charitable efforts. Punk's unapologetic activism showcases its commitment to challenging the status quo and advocating for a more equitable and just world.

Punk rock, with its raw and rebellious spirit, has played a significant role in amplifying dissent throughout its history. This subculture, born in the mid-1970s, emerged as a response to the social and political climate of its time. As we explore punk's role as a catalyst for dissent, we will uncover how the genre served as a powerful platform for raising awareness about societal and political issues. By examining key moments in punk history and iconic protest songs, we will shed light on the ways in which punk artists and fans have used the genre to challenge the status quo, addressing civil rights struggles, highlighting economic inequalities, and embodying the spirit of dissent.

Punk's amplification of dissent was not confined to abstract political discourse; it found tangible expression in its protest songs. These songs served as anthems for those who felt marginalized, oppressed, or simply disillusioned with the system. One iconic example is The Clash's "White Riot," a rallying cry against racial inequality and police brutality. The song's aggressive tone and confrontational lyrics captured the frustration and anger of marginalized communities, providing a voice for those who felt unheard.

Similarly, punk bands like Dead Kennedys addressed economic disparities and societal injustices. Their song "Holiday in Cambodia" critiqued the privileged elite and their lack of understanding of the struggles faced by the less fortunate. With biting satire and scathing commentary, punk bands like Dead Kennedys compelled listeners to confront uncomfortable truths about their society.

While punk's dissent often took the form of protest songs, it was also deeply rooted in its DIY (Do It Yourself) ethos. Punk encouraged self-reliance and self-expression, empowering bands and fans to take matters into their own hands. This self-empowerment extended to political activism, where punk's ethos of nonconformity and resistance translated into tangible action.

Benefit shows and charitable efforts became common within the punk community. Bands organized benefit concerts to support various social and political causes. The Dead Kennedys, for example, organized the "Rock Against Reagan" tour in the 1980s, which aimed to protest the policies of the Reagan administration. These concerts not only raised funds but also raised awareness about important issues, mobilizing punk fans to become actively engaged in social and political activism.

Environmentalism also found a home within the punk subculture. Punk bands, such as Bad Religion, addressed environmental issues in their music and used their platform to advocate for environmental protection. The "Rock for Nature" benefit concert series in the 1990s brought together punk and alternative rock bands to raise awareness about ecological concerns, demonstrating how punk's dissent extended to the environmental sphere.

**The Punk Community**

The punk community has long been a bastion of activism, where fans actively participate in promoting social change. Beyond being passionate music enthusiasts, punk fans often transform into activists, channelling their energy and dedication towards causes that align with the ethos of punk rock. In this section, we delve into the dynamic world of activism within the punk community, exploring the ways in which punk fans have rallied together to support various causes. Through anecdotes and examples, we reveal how the punk ethos transcends music, fostering a profound sense of social responsibility among its adherents.

As punk music gained momentum, so did the desire among fans to channel their passion into meaningful actions. Activism became an extension of the punk ethos, where the rejection of societal norms was not confined to lyrics or fashion but translated into tangible efforts to bring about change.

One of the most visible forms of activism within the punk community is the organization of benefit shows. These events serve a dual purpose: raising awareness about pressing issues and generating funds for specific causes. Benefit shows have been instrumental in mobilizing the punk community to support various social and political initiatives. Benefit shows also served as a rallying point for the punk community to address specific challenges faced by its members. In the early 1980s, the "Hunger Artists" benefit concerts were organized to address issues of hunger and homelessness within the punk community itself. This demonstrated the punk ethos of taking care of one's own, an extension of the "DIY or die" mentality.

Beyond benefit shows, punk fans have been active in creating grassroots initiatives to address societal problems. These initiatives are often characterized by their hands-on approach and direct impact on communities.

Food Not Bombs is a notable example of a grassroots initiative deeply rooted in the punk community. Founded in the early 1980s, it is an all-volunteer organization dedicated to feeding the hungry and protesting war and poverty. Food Not Bombs chapters have sprouted in cities worldwide, with punk fans often taking a lead role in these efforts. The organization's commitment to direct action and the redistribution of resources aligns closely with the punk ethos of challenging the status quo.

Similarly, housing cooperatives have been established within the punk community to address issues of affordable housing and homelessness. These cooperatives emphasize communal living and self-sufficiency, providing an alternative to traditional housing structures. Many punks have actively participated in and initiated such cooperative housing projects, embodying the punk spirit of self-reliance and social responsibility.

Punk activism is not limited to fundraising or volunteer work; it also involves direct action and protest. Punk fans often take to the streets to advocate for causes they are passionate about, using their collective voice to effect change. Punk activism of the 1970s tackled issues such as nuclear disarmament, feminism, LGBTQ+ rights, and racial equality.

Punk's spirit of dissent knows no bounds, transcending borders and generations. In the 1990s, the Riot Grrrl movement, led by feminist punk bands like Bikini Kill and Sleater-Kinney, fearlessly confronted gender inequality and sexual harassment. Through their music and activism, they challenged entrenched societal norms, both within and outside the punk scene. Riot Grrrl exemplified how punk fans can engage in direct action, addressing pressing issues like gender-based discrimination and empowering others through zines, workshops, and protest rallies.

Punk's impact on civil rights struggles has been significant. In the late 1970s and early 1980s, the Rock Against Racism (RAR) movement in the UK harnessed punk to combat racial tensions and far-right ideologies. Punk bands and fans organized concerts and protests that explicitly condemned racism and fascism, successfully raising awareness and fostering anti-racism unity.

Punk's role as a catalyst for dissent was not confined to the past; it continues to shape the genre and influence contemporary issues. More recently, punk fans have actively participated in protests against police brutality, racial injustice, and environmental crises. The Black Lives Matter protests following George Floyd's killing in 2020 saw strong support from the punk community, with bands and fans taking to the streets to demand racial equality and an end to police violence, reaffirming punk's commitment to social justice.

In the 1990s and early 2000s, the punk and DIY scenes were instrumental in raising awareness about global trade injustices and corporate exploitation. Bands like Anti-Flag and Propagandhi addressed these issues in their music and actively participated in protests against organizations like the World Trade Organization (WTO).

At the heart of activism within the punk community is the embodiment of the punk ethos, which encourages self-expression, nonconformity, and a steadfast commitment to social responsibility. Punk fans are driven by a desire to challenge authority, question societal norms, and actively participate in shaping a more equitable world. In the face of crises, punk fans are often at the forefront of mobilization. The punk ethos instils a sense of urgency and a call to action, pushing individuals to confront injustice head-on. It is a spirit that has fuelled countless protests, benefit shows, and grassroots initiatives aimed at making a difference in the lives of marginalized communities.

In conclusion, activism within the punk community is a testament to the genre's enduring commitment to social and political change. Emerging from a rejection of mainstream conformity, punk has consistently encouraged fans to channel their energy into meaningful actions. Benefit shows, grassroots initiatives, direct action, and protest have all been part of the punk community's efforts to raise awareness and address societal issues. Beyond the music, the punk ethos fosters a profound sense of social responsibility, driving fans to actively engage with the world and challenge the status quo. Punk remains a catalyst for dissent and a powerful force for positive change in society.

## Punk's Impact on Environmental Activism

The intersection of punk and environmental activism may not seem immediately obvious, but it represents a significant and meaningful chapter in the genre's history. While punk music is often associated with dissent, rebellion, and a rejection of societal norms, it has also evolved to address and engage with pressing issues such as environmental sustainability and climate change. In this section, we will explore how punk, as a cultural force, has extended its activist reach to address environmental concerns. We will examine the ways in which punk bands, fans, and the broader community have embraced environmentalism as an integral part of the punk ethos.

The roots of punk's engagement with environmentalism can be traced back to its broader ethos of dissent and rebellion. Punk emerged in the 1970s as a direct response to the societal and political issues of the time, ranging from economic instability to political disillusionment. Bands like The Ramones, The Sex Pistols, and The Clash became sonic revolutionaries, channelling the frustration and disillusionment of disaffected youth into music that challenged the status quo. While the early punk movement primarily focused on social and political issues, it laid the foundation for a broader range of concerns, including environmentalism, to become integral to the punk spirit.

The 1980s witnessed the emergence of a more explicit environmental consciousness within the punk community. This shift was partly a response to the growing global awareness of environmental issues, including pollution, deforestation, and climate change. Bands like Dead Kennedys and Crass began incorporating environmental themes into their lyrics, using their music as a means to raise awareness about ecological challenges. For example, Dead Kennedys' song "Riot" criticized the wastefulness of consumer culture and its impact on the environment, aligning with the broader punk critique of materialism and conformity. Meanwhile, Crass, known for their anarchic punk sound, also addressed environmental concerns in songs like "Reality Asylum," which condemned industrialization and its ecological consequences.

The marriage of punk activism and environmentalism gained momentum in the 1990s. During this decade, environmental issues increasingly dominated global discourse, with growing concerns about deforestation, endangered species, and climate change. Punk bands and fans began to align their activist efforts with these concerns, recognizing that environmental degradation was not only a threat to the planet but also a reflection of societal values that punk had long critiqued.

One of the most influential and pioneering figures in punk's engagement with environmentalism was Tim Armstrong, best known as a member of the bands Rancid and Operation Ivy. Armstrong's lyrics often addressed ecological themes, and he used his platform to raise awareness about the environment. In the song "East Bay Night," he laments the loss of natural beauty in the San Francisco Bay Area due to urbanization and development. Armstrong's commitment to environmentalism extended beyond music; he founded the clothing brand Eco-Logical, which promotes eco-friendly and sustainable fashion choices.

The punk community's embrace of environmentalism was not limited to individual artists. It manifested in collective efforts, such as the Punk Planet magazine's Green Issue in 1995. This special edition of the magazine was dedicated entirely to environmental issues and featured articles on topics like eco-activism, sustainable living, and the environmental impact of punk music itself. This initiative marked a significant moment in the convergence of punk and environmental activism, highlighting the punk community's capacity to engage meaningfully with ecological concerns.

Punk's commitment to environmentalism further materialized through a variety of initiatives and events. Punk shows and festivals became venues for raising awareness about ecological issues and fundraising for environmental causes. Benefit concerts, in particular, became a powerful tool for the punk community to support environmental organizations.

One notable example is the Punk Earth Summit, an event organized in 1990 by the band 7 Seconds. This summit brought together punk bands, environmental organizations, and fans for a series of concerts and workshops focused on environmental activism. The summit aimed to bridge the gap between punk culture and the environmental movement, emphasizing the interconnectedness of social and environmental justice issues.

As the 21st century progressed, punk's engagement with environmentalism continued to evolve. In 2003, the Vans Warped Tour, a popular traveling punk and alternative music festival, launched the Keep-A-Breast Foundation's Non-Toxic Revolution campaign. This initiative aimed to raise awareness about toxic chemicals in everyday products and promote healthier and more sustainable alternatives. The campaign featured educational booths at the festival, where attendees could learn about the impact of toxic substances on health and the environment.

The intersection of punk and environmentalism also gave rise to subgenres like "eco-punk," characterized by a heightened focus on ecological themes and sustainability. Bands within this subgenre often incorporate environmental messages into their lyrics, addressing issues such as deforestation, pollution, and climate change. Eco-punk serves as a powerful reminder of punk's capacity to evolve and adapt while remaining true to its activist roots.

Despite the positive strides made by the punk community in engaging with environmentalism, this intersection has not been without its challenges and critiques. Some have argued that punk's environmental activism is not always as sustainable as it appears, pointing out the environmental impact of touring, merchandise production, and the music industry as a whole. Others have raised concerns about the performative nature of some eco-punk bands, suggesting that their environmental messages may be insincere or tokenistic.

Nevertheless, punk's engagement with environmentalism remains a significant and evolving aspect of the genre's legacy. The willingness of punk artists and fans to address ecological concerns, raise awareness, and promote sustainable practices underscores the enduring spirit of dissent and activism that defines punk.

Punk's role as a catalyst for environmental activism exemplifies the genre's ability to adapt and respond to pressing social and ecological issues. From its early days of dissent and rebellion, punk has evolved to encompass a wide range of concerns, including those related to the environment. Through lyrics, initiatives, benefit shows, and eco-friendly practices, the punk community has embraced environmentalism as an integral part of its ethos. While challenges and critiques exist, the commitment of punk to raising awareness about ecological sustainability and climate change underscores its enduring legacy as a force for social and environmental change. In an era marked by urgent ecological challenges, punk continues to amplify the voices of those advocating for a more sustainable and just world.

# DIVISION.4-2

## A Taste of Subgenres: Anarchy, Chaos, & Integrity

### Anarcho-Punk

In the sprawling landscape of punk, there exists a subgenre that stands as a potent fusion of music and political activism — anarcho-punk. This subsection takes us on a journey into the heart of anarcho-punk, exploring its origins, key characteristics, and the influential bands that wielded their music as a weapon for political dissent and change. Anarcho-punk was not merely a style of music; it was a fervent rebellion against authority, capitalism, and the status quo, making it a distinct and formidable force within the punk movement.

To understand anarcho-punk, we must delve into its origins. Anarcho-punk emerged in the late 1970s and early 1980s. It was a direct reaction to what many saw as a co-optation of the punk ethos by mainstream media and record labels. The punk rebellion had not lost its fire, but it had evolved. Anarcho-punk, with its uncompromising stance on political and social issues, emerged as a vanguard of this evolving punk spirit.

Anarcho-punk distinguished itself through a set of key characteristics that set it apart from other punk subgenres. Musically, it often featured aggressive and raw soundscapes, with bands opting for a lo-fi and DIY aesthetic. Lyrics were a crucial component, addressing a wide spectrum of political and societal issues, including anarchism, anti-capitalism, anti-fascism, and anti-authoritarianism. Anarcho-punk was defined by its fierce independence, rejecting the trappings of mainstream music production and embracing the DIY ethos wholeheartedly. Bands produced their music, organized their tours, and disseminated their messages independently, reflecting the punk spirit of self-reliance and autonomy.

Anarcho-punk's most distinctive feature was its unwavering commitment to political activism. It wasn't enough for anarcho-punk bands to simply play music; they saw their music as a vehicle for disseminating messages of resistance and revolution. One of the most iconic anarcho-punk bands, Crass, epitomized this ethos. Formed in 1977, Crass was not only known for their confrontational sound but also for their provocative lyrics and uncompromising political stance.

Crass's debut album, "The Feeding of the 5000," featured the track "Asylum," which directly challenged the system's treatment of mental health patients. It was a searing indictment of the dehumanization and mistreatment of vulnerable individuals within institutional settings. Crass's music was a call to arms, urging listeners to question the world around them and take a stand against oppression.

Another seminal anarcho-punk band, Discharge, made waves with their distinctive d-beat sound and uncompromising lyrics. The band's 1982 album, "Hear Nothing See Nothing Say Nothing," is considered a landmark in anarcho-punk history. The album's title track, "Hear Nothing See Nothing Say Nothing," is a blistering critique of political apathy and a rallying cry for resistance against oppressive regimes.

Discharge's music was characterized by its relentless speed and ferocity, which perfectly mirrored the urgency of their political messages. Songs like "Protest and Survive" addressed nuclear disarmament, while "State Violence, State Control" tackled police brutality and the abuse of power. Discharge's music was a sonic weapon against injustice, and their uncompromising stance made them icons of the anarcho-punk movement.

The impact of anarcho-punk extended far beyond the shores of the United Kingdom, where it originated. The genre resonated with disaffected youth around the world who were seeking a voice against the injustices they perceived in their societies. Bands like Dead Kennedys in the United States and Subhumans in Canada embraced anarcho-punk's ethos of resistance, blending it with their own regional perspectives on political activism and societal critique.

The global reach of anarcho-punk exemplified its universality as a form of sonic rebellion. It transcended national boundaries and connected like-minded individuals who were united by a common desire for change and a refusal to accept the status quo.

As we delve into the history of anarcho-punk, it becomes evident that this subgenre was more than just a style of music; it was a movement driven by a passionate commitment to political activism. Bands like Crass and Discharge, among many others, used their music as a platform to challenge oppressive systems, call for social justice, and empower listeners to question authority.

The legacy of anarcho-punk endures today, as its spirit lives on in the music of contemporary punk bands who continue to use their lyrics and sound to confront pressing political and societal issues. Anarcho-punk serves as a powerful reminder that music has the potential to be a catalyst for social change and a rallying cry for those who refuse to remain silent in the face of injustice. In this way, anarcho-punk stands as a testament to the enduring power of music as a force for dissent and activism.

### Crust Punk: Chaos and Activism

Within the sprawling and diverse punk landscape, one subgenre stands out for its raw intensity, chaotic soundscapes, and unrelenting commitment to political activism – crust punk. This subsection embarks on a journey through the chaotic world of crust punk, exploring its defining characteristics, its deep connection to socio-political messages, and the notable bands that have left an indelible mark on the punk genre. Crust punk emerged as a testament to the punk spirit's ability to channel anger, frustration, and dissent into a sonic revolution.

Crust punk is often characterized by its sonic chaos and unapologetic intensity. The genre's music is characterized by its fierce speed, aggressive guitar riffs, and a distinctive vocal style that often includes guttural, shouted, or growled vocals. The production values are typically raw and unpolished, emphasizing the DIY ethos that is integral to punk culture.

Lyrically, crust punk is deeply rooted in political and social themes. Songs address a wide array of issues, including environmental degradation, anti-authoritarianism, class struggle, and anti-capitalism. The lyrics are often confrontational and provocative, reflecting a desire to challenge the status quo and provoke thought and action. Crust punk is a genre that thrives on chaos, both musically and thematically, using its sonic ferocity as a vehicle for activism.

### Amebix

To understand the essence of crust punk, we must first examine one of its pioneering bands, Amebix. Formed in England in the late 1970s, Amebix was instrumental in shaping the sound and ethos of crust punk. Their debut album, "Arise!" released in 1985, is considered a seminal work within the genre.

Amebix's music was characterized by its thunderous, apocalyptic sound. Tracks like "The Moor" and "Axeman" conveyed a sense of impending doom, mirroring the disillusionment and frustration felt by many during the turbulent socio-political climate of the 1980s. The band's lyrics were a fierce critique of authority, environmental destruction, and societal decay.

### Doom

Another band that deserves recognition within the crust punk realm is Doom. Hailing from the United Kingdom, Doom emerged in the early 1980s as part of the anarcho-punk movement. However, their sound was deeply rooted in the chaotic and aggressive style that would later become synonymous with crust punk.

Doom's music was fast, furious, and unrelenting. Songs like "Police Bastard" and "Bury the Debt (Not the Dead)" were anthems of anti-authoritarianism and social protest. Doom's lyrics were a searing indictment of the police state, economic inequality, and the exploitation of the working class. The band's music embodied the rage and frustration of those who saw the world's injustices and refused to remain silent.

**Fusing Chaos and Activism**

Crust punk's fusion of chaotic music and political activism was not limited to a specific time or place; it became a global phenomenon. Bands from various corners of the world adopted the genre's ethos and added their regional perspectives on political and social issues. Crust punk provided a unifying platform for individuals who were united by a shared desire for change and a refusal to accept the injustices they saw in their societies.

One of the defining characteristics of crust punk is its direct and unfiltered approach to politics. Unlike some other punk subgenres that may couch political messages in metaphor or allegory, crust punk often confronts issues head-on. Whether addressing environmental destruction, corporate greed, or state oppression, crust punk lyrics are a call to action. The genre's music serves as a rallying cry for those who refuse to remain passive in the face of injustice.

The legacy of crust punk endures in the contemporary punk landscape, as its spirit lives on in bands that continue to use their music as a vehicle for political dissent and activism. Crust punk has demonstrated that music can be more than just entertainment; it can be a powerful means of challenging oppressive systems, amplifying marginalized voices, and inspiring individuals to take a stand for justice.

In conclusion, crust punk stands as a testament to the enduring power of punk rock to channel chaos into activism. Its aggressive sound, confrontational lyrics, and unrelenting commitment to political change have left an indelible mark on the punk genre and continue to inspire generations of punk musicians and activists. Crust punk reminds us that music can be a force for dissent and a call to action, and that the spirit of rebellion remains alive and well within the punk community.

**Sobriety and Integrity**

In the multifaceted realm of punk rock, where rebellion and subversion reign supreme, there exists a lesser-explored but profoundly impactful dimension – sobriety and integrity. This subsection embarks on a journey into the heart of the punk subculture, where the do-it-yourself (DIY) ethos is not only a hallmark but also a vehicle for rejecting mainstream norms around alcohol and substance use. Here, we uncover the significance of sobriety and integrity within punk, exploring how bands and fans alike have embraced authenticity and ethical values as an essential part of the punk spirit.

At the core of the punk movement lies the DIY ethos, a guiding principle that encourages individuals to take matters into their own hands, from creating their music and zines to organizing shows and living spaces. This ethos was instrumental in fostering the sobriety and integrity aspects of punk. Rejecting the corporate machinery of the music industry, punks carved out their own spaces where creativity flourished, and ethical values thrived.

The DIY ethos extended to issues of sobriety, as many punks rejected the mainstream culture of alcohol and substance use. This rejection was not merely a moral stance but also a means of preserving the authenticity and autonomy of the punk subculture. By avoiding the trappings of addiction and commercial exploitation, punks maintained a clear and unadulterated channel for their creativity and activism.

Numerous punk bands exemplify the commitment to sobriety and integrity, using their music and platform to challenge societal norms around substance use. One notable band that deserves recognition in this context is Minor Threat. Hailing from Washington, D.C., Minor Threat is often credited with pioneering the straight edge movement, which advocates for a drug-free and sober lifestyle.

Minor Threat's song "Straight Edge," released in 1981, became an anthem for those who rejected the excesses of alcohol and drug culture. It resonated with a generation that sought clarity and consciousness in a world clouded by intoxication. Minor Threat's commitment to sobriety was not just a personal choice; it was a message to their fans that they could pursue an authentic and sober life while still challenging the status quo.

The DIY ethos extended beyond the music itself, shaping the spaces where punk culture thrived. DIY venues became hubs for the punk community, places where bands could perform and fans could congregate. These spaces were often characterized by their substance-free policies, which not only aligned with the sobriety aspect of punk but also created safer and more inclusive environments for all attendees.

DIY venues were not just about music; they were about fostering a sense of belonging and shared values. The rejection of alcohol and substance use in these spaces was a declaration of independence from mainstream entertainment industries, which often profited from the sale of intoxicants at shows. By creating substance-free spaces, punks ensured that their gatherings remained authentic expressions of their culture and beliefs.

The legacy of sobriety and integrity in punk endures, inspiring successive generations of punks to prioritize authenticity and ethical values. Bands like Fugazi, a post-hardcore outfit formed in the late 1980s, continued to champion sobriety and integrity as integral aspects of their music and ethos. Fugazi's commitment to keeping ticket prices low, avoiding corporate sponsors, and advocating for social and political causes embodied the punk spirit of independence and integrity.

Sobriety and integrity in punk continue to manifest in various forms. Punk festivals and DIY spaces around the world often maintain substance-free policies, ensuring that punk remains a welcoming and inclusive subculture. Moreover, punk bands continue to address issues of addiction, mental health, and ethical values in their lyrics, providing a platform for fans to engage with these critical topics.

Sobriety and integrity are not mere afterthoughts within the punk subculture; they are integral components of its ethos. The DIY ethos that underpins punk has provided a fertile ground for rejecting mainstream norms around alcohol and substance use, creating spaces where authenticity and ethical values thrive. Bands like Minor Threat and Fugazi have left an indelible mark, not only with their music but also with their unwavering commitment to sobriety and integrity.

The legacy of sobriety and integrity in punk endures, reminding us that punk is not just a genre of music but a way of life rooted in challenging the status quo, preserving authenticity, and upholding ethical values. As long as there are voices of dissent and a desire for change, the punk spirit of sobriety and integrity will continue to shine as a beacon of authenticity in a world often marred by excess and exploitation.

**Fight for Equality/Inclusivity: Gender, Feminism & LGBTQ+ in Punk**

In this section, we embark on a transformative journey through the punk landscape, where the fight for equality and inclusivity takes centre stage. The punk subculture, often associated with rebellion and nonconformity, serves as a fertile ground for challenging traditional norms related to gender and sexuality. We delve into the evolution of punk's approach to LGBTQ+ issues, gender roles, the role of women, and the intertwined threads of feminism, exploring how punk has both mirrored and contributed to broader social changes.

Punk, from its very inception, has challenged conventional norms and classifications, including those related to gender and identity. Punk's emphasis on individualism and authenticity has paved the way for gender fluidity and nonconformity to flourish within the subculture.

One significant figure in the early punk scene who defied gender norms was Jayne County. Known as the "rock transgender pioneer," County's confrontational performances and fearless expression blazed a trail for transgender individuals within the punk world. Her song "Man Enough to Be a Woman" challenged the binary constraints of gender and became an anthem of gender nonconformity within punk.

As punk evolved, artists like Patti Smith and Poly Styrene (of X-Ray Spex) pushed against traditional expectations of femininity, offering alternative models of female empowerment. Their lyrics and personas defied the limitations imposed on women in the music industry and society at large.

The punk movement's embrace of LGBTQ+ individuals and issues has evolved over time, reflecting broader societal changes. In the early days of punk, LGBTQ+ themes were often implicit rather than explicit, as artists like Lou Reed explored themes of sexual fluidity in their lyrics.

However, as LGBTQ+ rights gained momentum in the late 20th century, punk became increasingly intertwined with the LGBTQ+ revolution. Bands like Pansy Division emerged, openly celebrating queer sexuality in their music and challenging heteronormative norms. Songs like "Homo Christmas" and "Fem in a Black Leather Jacket" provided anthems of empowerment for LGBTQ+ punks.

The riot grrrl movement, which emerged in the early 1990s and is closely associated with feminism, provided another platform for queer voices in punk. Bands like Bikini Kill and Sleater-Kinney not only addressed issues of gender equality but also celebrated LGBTQ+ identities. Riot grrrl zines and publications often featured discussions of queer politics and visibility.

Queercore, a subgenre of punk, emerged in the 1980s and played a pivotal role in confronting heteronormative attitudes within punk and society at large. Bands like The Dicks and Team Dresch openly identified as queer and used their music to challenge assumptions about sexual orientation.

One of the most influential figures in queercore was Bruce LaBruce, a filmmaker and musician who co-authored the manifesto for the movement. LaBruce's band, The Queercore Punx, promoted a DIY ethos that rejected commercialization and corporate influence. The movement emphasized the importance of queer visibility and self-expression, pushing back against societal expectations.

**Women in Punk: From Pioneers to Empowerment**

The role of women in punk has evolved significantly since the genre's inception. While punk's early years saw a scarcity of female musicians in prominent positions, several trailblazers shattered those barriers.

Patti Smith, often referred to as the "Godmother of Punk," paved the way for women in the genre with her fearless performances and thought-provoking lyrics. Her debut album, "Horses," remains a seminal work in punk history, challenging preconceived notions of what women could achieve in music.

The Riot Grrrl movement of the 1990s marked a turning point for women in punk. Bands like Bikini Kill, Bratmobile, and L7 not only created music but also established a feminist subculture that addressed issues of sexual assault, consent, and women's empowerment. Riot grrrl zines, such as "Jigsaw" and "Girl Germs," provided a platform for women's voices and experiences.

Feminism has been a driving force within punk, pushing for gender equality and addressing issues of misogyny and sexism within the scene. Riot grrrl bands were at the forefront of this movement, using their music and activism to challenge patriarchal norms. Songs like Bikini Kill's "Rebel Girl" celebrated female friendship and solidarity.

Beyond riot grrrl, feminism continues to be a central theme within punk. Bands like Sleater-Kinney and Le Tigre explore feminist themes in their lyrics, addressing topics such as body image, reproductive rights, and women's agency. These bands have provided a platform for discussions about feminism and gender equality within and beyond the punk scene.

In conclusion, punk's engagement with LGBTQ+ issues, gender nonconformity, and feminism exemplifies its commitment to challenging societal norms and promoting inclusivity. From the early pioneers like Jayne County and Patti Smith to the riot grrrls and contemporary bands, punk has continuously evolved as a space where fluid identities, feminism, and LGBTQ+ rights are not just discussed but celebrated.

Punk's influence extends beyond music; it has played a crucial role in the broader struggle for gender equality and LGBTQ+ rights. By embracing these issues, punk has demonstrated that it is more than a genre; it is a transformative force that empowers individuals to express their true selves, challenge oppressive norms, and create a more inclusive world. In a world that often marginalizes and discriminates, punk stands as a beacon of resistance, acceptance, and empowerment.

# LAST.TRACK.

This chapter has been a deep dive into the heart of punk's engagement with activism, politics, and society. It has unveiled the multifaceted ways in which punk transcends its musical boundaries to serve as a powerful catalyst for change and a voice of dissent. From its origins in the defiant spirit of anarchy to its robust involvement in environmentalism and LGBTQ+ rights, punk has consistently defied conventions and embraced issues of social relevance.

The chapter commenced by tracing punk's origins in anarchy, revealing how the rejection of societal norms has been at the core of the punk spirit. We explored how punk's raw, unfiltered music served as a sonic rebellion against the status quo, with bands like The Clash and The Sex Pistols amplifying dissent and challenging established authority. Punk's impact on civil rights struggles and its role in contemporary protests against police brutality illustrated its enduring commitment to addressing societal injustices.

The exploration of sobriety and integrity within the punk community demonstrated how the genre fosters authenticity and ethical values. Rejecting mainstream norms around substance use, punk bands and fans embraced the do-it-yourself (DIY) ethos, emphasizing self-reliance and autonomy. In doing so, they created a subculture that values personal integrity and resists conformity to societal expectations.

The chapter continued by shining a spotlight on gender, feminism, and LGBTQ+ issues in punk. Punk's celebration of nonconformity and individualism has been epitomized by its embrace of gender fluidity and nonconformity. It has provided a platform for LGBTQ+ individuals to challenge heteronormative attitudes and promote queer visibility. The riot grrrl movement and queercore subgenre have exemplified punk's commitment to inclusivity and challenging traditional gender roles.

We explored punk's engagement with environmentalism, showcasing how punk has expanded its activist reach to address pressing ecological concerns. Through lyrics, initiatives, and collaborations, punk has demonstrated its commitment to advocating for ecological sustainability and raising awareness about climate change.

In conclusion, we have uncovered the dynamic intersection of punk, activism, politics, and society. Punk's sonic rebellion, its embrace of sobriety and integrity, and its dedication to gender equality, LGBTQ+ rights, and environmental activism highlight its enduring relevance as a force for change. Punk serves as a constant reminder that music can be a catalyst for social and political transformation, providing a space for dissent, expression, and empowerment. As we continue to explore the rich tapestry of punk's impact, it is clear that the genre's legacy is one of resilience, inclusivity, and a relentless pursuit of a more just and compassionate world. Punk remains a vibrant and vital voice for those who refuse to conform, and its resonance continues to reverberate through the corridors of activism, politics, and society.

# DIVISION.5

## Passing the Molotov: A Punk Relay

The 1980s marked a pivotal period in the history of punk music. Following the explosive rise and fall of bands like the Sex Pistols and the Clash in the late 1970s, many wondered if punk could maintain its rebellious spirit and grassroots ethos. However, far from fizzling out, punk experienced a remarkable resurgence during this decade, evolving in new directions and reinvigorating its message.

In this chapter, we embark on a journey through the 80s and into the early 90s, a time when punk was far from dead but, in fact, thriving with a renewed sense of purpose. This was an era that witnessed the emergence of influential bands and subgenres, the growth of regional punk scenes, and a recommitment to punk's DIY (Do It Yourself) ethic.

The punk revival of the 80s was not just a nostalgic return to punk's roots; it was a dynamic and multifaceted movement that expanded the boundaries of punk music and culture. Bands like Bad Religion, Suicidal Tendencies, and The Adolescents emerged as pioneers of this revival, taking punk in fresh and exciting directions.

As we explore this period, we'll delve into the stories of key bands and scenes that played pivotal roles in punk's resurgence. From the politically charged anthems of Dead Kennedys to the SoCal punk explosion led by The Offspring and their contemporaries, we'll dissect the various facets of punk during these transformative years.

While the chapter pays homage to the pioneers of the punk revival, it also explores the complex relationships and controversies within the punk community during this time. Bands like Green Day and Blink-182, initially embraced as part of the underground scene, faced accusations of "selling out" as their music reached mainstream audiences.

Furthermore, this chapter reflects on the enduring legacy of the 80s and early 90s punk revival. The bands that emerged during this period continue to influence contemporary music, serving as a bridge between the original punk era and the vibrant punk landscape of today.

As we navigate through this chapter, we'll witness how punk, far from fading into obscurity, reinvented itself, evolved, and thrived. It's a testament to the resilience of a genre born from the streets and its enduring ability to defy conventions, confront injustices, and inspire generations of rebels and misfits worldwide. So, let's embark on this journey through the punk revival of the 80s and early 90s, where the spirit of punk burned brighter than ever.

# DIVISION.5-1

## The Pioneers of Punk Revival

In the late 1970s, the punk scene was at a crossroads. The initial shockwaves sent by bands like the Sex Pistols, The Clash, and the Ramones had reverberated around the world, inspiring countless musicians to pick up instruments and join the burgeoning punk movement. However, by the end of the decade, the Sex Pistols had imploded, and the punk movement faced questions about its future. It was during this critical juncture that a new wave of punk pioneers emerged, reigniting the flames of rebellion and creativity that defined the genre. Bands like Bad Religion, Suicidal Tendencies, The Adolescents, and The Vandals played a pivotal role in revitalizing the punk scene, each with its unique sound and lyrical approach.

## The Emergence of Bad Religion

Bad Religion's origins can be traced back to 1980 when high school friends Greg Graffin and Brett Gurewitz decided to form a band in Southern California. Drawing inspiration from the original punk movement, they incorporated melodic elements into their music, creating a distinctive sound characterized by fast-paced guitar riffs and thought-provoking lyrics. Bad Religion's early music resonated with disaffected youth, addressing themes of alienation and societal disillusionment. Their debut album, "How Could Hell Be Any Worse?" released in 1982, exemplified the band's blend of punk aggression and melody. Tracks like "We're Only Gonna Die" and "Fuck Armageddon... This is Hell" showcased their social commentary and lyrical depth. Bad Religion's emergence marked a return to punk's intellectual and introspective roots, setting the stage for a new era of punk music.

## The Suicidal Tendencies Phenomenon

While punk was characterized by a raw, rebellious energy, Suicidal Tendencies introduced a new dimension to the genre. Formed in Venice, California, in 1980, the band was fronted by the enigmatic Mike Muir, whose intense and confrontational stage presence set them apart. Suicidal Tendencies blended punk with elements of hardcore, thrash, and metal, creating a unique fusion that appealed to a diverse audience. Their self-titled debut album, released in 1983, included iconic tracks like "Institutionalized" and "I Saw Your Mommy," which showcased the band's genre-bending approach and Muir's biting social commentary. Suicidal Tendencies' music captured the frustration and angst of youth culture, reflecting the tensions and disillusionment of the early 1980s.

## The Adolescents: Youthful Rebellion

Hailing from Fullerton, California, The Adolescents embodied the spirit of youthful rebellion that had fuelled punk from its inception. Formed in 1980, the band comprised teenagers whose raw energy and unapologetic attitude translated into their music. Their self-titled debut album, released in 1981, was a frenetic burst of punk anthems. Tracks like "Amoeba" and "Kids of the Black Hole" captured the exuberance and defiance of adolescence, resonating with a generation of young punks. The Adolescents' contribution to the punk revival was not only musical but also cultural, as they embodied the do-it-yourself (DIY) ethos that had been a cornerstone of punk since its inception.

## The Vandals: A Touch of Irreverence

The Vandals, another Southern California punk outfit, injected a healthy dose of irreverence and humour into the punk revival. Formed in 1980, the band's early years were marked by lineup changes, but they solidified their sound by the mid-1980s. The Vandals' music was characterized by catchy melodies, witty lyrics, and a tongue-in-cheek approach to punk. Their 1982 album "Peace Thru Vandalism" and subsequent releases like "When in Rome Do as the Vandals" (1984) and "Slippery When Ill" (1989) showcased their knack for humour and satire. Tracks like "Urban Struggle" and "Anarchy Burger (Hold the Government)" were humorous critiques of punk's own rebellious clichés. The Vandals' contribution to the punk revival was a reminder that punk could be fun, light-hearted, and a vehicle for social commentary, all at the same time.

### Revitalizing the Punk Scene

These pioneering bands breathed new life into the punk scene during a period of uncertainty and change. As the Sex Pistols disbanded, and the original punk movement faced challenges, Bad Religion, Suicidal Tendencies, The Adolescents, and The Vandals emerged as torchbearers of punk's core values. They maintained punk's DIY ethos, emphasizing self-expression, individuality, and resistance against societal norms. Their music resonated with a new generation of fans while simultaneously appealing to those who had been part of punk's early years.

Moreover, these bands represented the diversity within punk. Bad Religion's melodic punk sound offered a departure from the raw aggression of hardcore punk, while Suicidal Tendencies brought a fusion of genres that expanded the boundaries of what punk could be. The Adolescents embodied the youthful spirit of rebellion, and The Vandals injected humour and satire

# DIVISION.5-2

### The Punk Explosion

The mid to late 1980s marked a significant turning point in the history of punk music. During this period, the punk scene experienced a remarkable proliferation of bands and subgenres, expanding its reach and influence. It was an era characterized by diversity, experimentation, and the emergence of bands that would go on to become iconic figures in the punk landscape. Among these influential acts were Rancid, NOFX, Dead Kennedys, and Pennywise, each of which contributed to the evolution of punk music and left an indelible mark on both the punk scene and the broader musical landscape.

The mid-1980s saw punk music branching out into an array of subgenres, each with its unique style and thematic focus. Hardcore punk, characterized by its blistering tempo and aggressive sound, continued to thrive, with bands like Minor Threat and Black Flag leading the charge. At the same time, punk began to evolve into new directions. Post-punk and alternative punk acts like Hüsker Dü and The Replacements introduced more melodic and experimental elements into the genre.

This period also witnessed the emergence of skate punk, a subgenre closely associated with the skateboarding culture of the time. Skate punk bands, while still maintaining the raw energy of punk, often incorporated elements of surf rock and garage punk, creating a distinct sonic identity. As a result, the punk scene diversified, appealing to a broader audience while retaining its rebellious spirit.

### Rancid: The East Bay Pioneers

One of the standout bands of this era was Rancid, hailing from the San Francisco Bay Area. Formed in 1991, Rancid was a product of the punk and hardcore scenes of the East Bay. Comprising members who had previously played in bands like Operation Ivy and Downfall, Rancid brought a unique blend of punk, ska, and reggae influences to their music. Their self-titled debut album, released in 1993, showcased their signature sound, characterized by catchy guitar riffs, anthemic choruses, and socially conscious lyrics.

Rancid's impact on the punk scene was profound. They revitalized the ska-punk subgenre, infusing it with a newfound energy that resonated with fans across the globe. Tracks like "Time Bomb" and "Ruby Soho" became punk anthems, solidifying Rancid's place as one of the leading bands of the punk revival. Rancid's success demonstrated that punk could evolve while staying true to its roots, appealing to both long-time punks and new generations of fans.

## NOFX: Punk's Unfiltered Voice

NOFX, a band known for its irreverent humour and unfiltered lyrics, was another influential figure in the punk explosion of the mid to late 1980s. Formed in Los Angeles in 1983, NOFX's music was characterized by its high-speed punk sound and witty, satirical lyrics. The band's 1988 album "White Trash, Two Heebs and a Bean" encapsulated their style, blending humour, social commentary, and unapologetic punk ethos.

NOFX's independent approach to punk music, including self-releasing many of their albums, resonated with the DIY spirit of the genre. Their lyrics tackled a range of topics, from politics to personal experiences, often with a humorous and sardonic twist. Tracks like "Linoleum" and "Don't Call Me White" became punk classics, embodying the band's unfiltered approach to songwriting.

## Dead Kennedys: Political Punk Pioneers

The Dead Kennedys, formed in San Francisco in 1978, were among the pioneers of political punk, a subgenre that used punk music as a platform for social and political critique. The band's music combined ferocious punk rock with biting satire and commentary. Dead Kennedys' frontman, Jello Biafra, was known for his provocative lyrics and theatrical stage presence.

Their debut album from 1980, "Fresh Fruit for Rotting Vegetables," marked a significant milestone in the punk milieu. With tracks such as "California Über Alles" and "Holiday in Cambodia," the songs delivered a sharp critique of political figures and societal conventions, delving into matters like compliance, authoritarianism, and the excesses of consumer culture. The Dead Kennedys' music and outspokenness made them icons of political punk, inspiring subsequent generations of punk bands to engage with social and political issues.

## Pennywise: The Hermosa Beach Soundtrack

Pennywise, formed in Hermosa Beach, California, in 1988, played a crucial role in the propagation of melodic hardcore punk during this era. Their self-titled debut album, released in 1991, showcased their distinctive blend of high-energy punk rock with melodic hooks. Pennywise's music was anthemic, reflecting the concerns and frustrations of the suburban youth culture of the time.

Tracks like "Bro Hymn" and "Unknown Road" became staples of the punk scene, serving as anthems for a generation searching for identity and meaning. Pennywise's lyrics often delved into themes of self-discovery, unity, and resistance. Their contribution to punk's melodic hardcore subgenre helped shape the sound of punk in the 1990s and beyond.

### The Impact on the Punk Scene and Mainstream Music

The bands of the mid to late 1980s punk explosion played a pivotal role in shaping the punk scene and influencing the broader music industry. Rancid's fusion of punk and ska breathed new life into the genre, paving the way for ska-punk bands like Less Than Jake and The Mighty Mighty Bosstones. NOFX's humorous and unfiltered approach provided a counterpoint to punk's more serious political and social themes. Dead Kennedys' politically charged music inspired generations of punk bands to engage with critical issues, and Pennywise's melodic hardcore sound offered a bridge between punk's aggression and accessibility.

Moreover, these bands contributed to the crossover of punk into mainstream music. While still rooted in the underground, punk began to make inroads into mainstream consciousness. Rancid, in particular, achieved mainstream success with albums like "And Out Come the Wolves," introducing punk to a wider audience without compromising its ethos. This period set the stage for punk's continued evolution and expansion, as bands like Rancid, NOFX, Dead Kennedys, and Pennywise showcased the genre's adaptability and enduring relevance.

In conclusion, the mid to late 1980s was a period of remarkable growth and diversification for punk music. Bands like Rancid, NOFX, Dead Kennedys, and Pennywise were instrumental in this transformation, each contributing a unique sound and lyrical perspective to the genre. Their influence extended beyond the punk scene, helping to define the sound of punk in the 1990s and paving the way for the genre's continued evolution in the mainstream music industry. This era stands as a testament to the enduring power of punk music to adapt, diversify, and inspire new generations of fans and musicians.

# DIVISION.5-3

## The SoCal Punk Phenomenon

The late 1980s and early 1990s witnessed the emergence of a vibrant and influential punk scene in Southern California (SoCal). This region became a hotbed of punk activity, producing a plethora of bands that played pivotal roles in shaping the punk revival during this period. Bands such as The Offspring, Lagwagon, Guttermouth, and No Use for a Name became synonymous with the SoCal punk sound, characterized by its blend of punk aggression, melodic hooks, and a distinct Southern California ethos.

## The Offspring

The SoCal punk scene of the late 1980s and early 1990s was defined by its fusion of punk's rebellious spirit with the laid-back, sun-soaked culture of Southern California. One of the standout bands of this scene was The Offspring, formed in 1984 in Garden Grove, California. Initially part of the underground punk circuit, The Offspring's journey to mainstream success was marked by dedication and perseverance.

The Offspring's early albums, such as "The Offspring" (1989) and "Ignition" (1992), showcased their distinctive sound, characterized by catchy melodies and Dexter Holland's distinctive vocals. However, it was their 1994 release, "Smash," that catapulted them to fame. With hit singles like "Self Esteem" and "Come Out and Play," "Smash" became an unexpected commercial success. The album's fusion of punk aggression and melodic hooks resonated with a broad audience, making it one of the best-selling independent albums of all time.

The Offspring's rise to prominence epitomized the SoCal punk phenomenon. Their music embodied the carefree and energetic spirit of Southern California, drawing fans from diverse backgrounds. Despite their mainstream success, The Offspring remained rooted in punk's DIY ethos and continued to address societal issues in their lyrics.

## Lagwagon, Guttermouth, No Use for a Name: SoCal Punk Diversity

The SoCal punk scene of the late 1980s and early 1990s was not limited to one particular style; instead, it encompassed a wide spectrum of sounds and themes. Bands like Lagwagon, Guttermouth, and No Use for a Name contributed to this diversity while staying true to the punk ethos.

**Lagwagon**, formed in 1989 in Goleta, California, brought a more melodic and technical approach to punk rock. Their 1992 album "Duh" and subsequent releases featured intricate guitar work and thought-provoking lyrics. Lagwagon's music appealed to punk fans with an appreciation for musicianship and depth in songwriting.

**Guttermouth**, from Huntington Beach, was known for its brash and irreverent style. Their music was characterized by fast-paced tempos, humorous lyrics, and a satirical take on punk culture. Guttermouth's antics and provocative stage presence stirred both amusement and controversy within the punk community.

**No Use for a Name**, led by the late Tony Sly, brought an emotional and introspective dimension to SoCal punk. Their 1993 album "The Daily Grind" showcased Sly's songwriting talent and the band's ability to blend punk intensity with heartfelt melodies. No Use for a Name's music resonated with those who sought a more introspective and emotive side of punk.

## Shaping the Punk Revival: SoCal's Impact

The SoCal punk phenomenon of the late 1980s and early 1990s played a pivotal role in shaping the punk revival during this period. Bands like The Offspring, Lagwagon, Guttermouth, and No Use for a Name brought a sense of vitality and innovation to the punk scene. Their music resonated with a generation of fans eager for an alternative to the prevailing musical trends of the time.

One of the key aspects of SoCal punk's influence was its ability to attract a diverse audience. The catchy melodies and relatable lyrics of bands like The Offspring made punk accessible to a broader demographic, ushering in new fans who may not have previously engaged with the genre. This expansion of the punk audience helped revitalize the scene and contributed to its enduring relevance.

The rise of SoCal punk was not without controversies and debates within the punk community. As some bands, including The Offspring, achieved mainstream success, questions arose about whether they had compromised their punk authenticity. The punk ethos of rebellion against the mainstream clashed with the commercial recognition these bands received.

Critics within the punk scene argued that mainstream success led to a dilution of the genre's rebellious spirit. Accusations of "selling out" were levelled at bands that signed with major record labels or altered their sound to appeal to a wider audience. These debates highlighted the tension between staying true to punk's DIY roots and the allure of greater exposure and resources that came with commercial success.

In conclusion, the SoCal punk phenomenon of the late 1980s and early 1990s left an indelible mark on the punk music scene and the broader music industry. Bands like The Offspring, Lagwagon, Guttermouth, and No Use for a Name showcased the diversity of punk music and attracted a wide range of fans. Their impact helped fuel the punk revival of the era, although not without sparking debates about authenticity and commercialization within the punk community. Ultimately, the SoCal punk scene of this period represents a dynamic and influential chapter in the history of punk music.

# DIVISION.5-4

### Punk's Hardcore Roots

The late 1980s and early 1990s witnessed the continued evolution of punk, with the emergence of the hardcore punk movement playing a significant role in reshaping the genre. Bands like Sick of It All, Ten Foot Pole, and even Green Day contributed to this movement, infusing it with their unique styles and perspectives. This section explores the hardcore punk scene during this period, delving into its roots, evolution, and impact on the broader punk revival.

Hardcore punk, as a subgenre, can trace its roots to the late 1970s and early 1980s, particularly in cities like Washington, D.C., and Los Angeles. However, by the late 1980s, hardcore had evolved, and its sound and ethos had become more distinct. This era saw a burgeoning scene of hardcore punk bands across the United States, each contributing to the evolution of the genre.

### Sick of It All: NYC Hardcore Pioneers

Sick of It All, hailing from New York City, was one of the prominent bands that epitomized the hardcore punk sound of the late 80s and early 90s. Formed in 1986, they drew from the energy of New York's punk and hardcore scenes. Their music was characterized by aggressive, fast-paced rhythms, shouted vocals, and lyrics that often delved into socio-political themes.

Sick of It All's 1989 debut album, "Blood, Sweat, and No Tears," encapsulated the spirit of hardcore punk during this period. Tracks like "Clobberin' Time" and "Injustice System!" resonated with fans who sought the cathartic release of hardcore music. The band's DIY ethos, touring relentlessly, and connecting with fans on a personal level contributed to their enduring influence within the hardcore punk scene.

### Ten Foot Pole: Melodic Hardcore

Ten Foot Pole, initially known as Scared Straight, emerged from the Southern California punk scene in the late 1980s. They offered a different take on hardcore, infusing it with melodic elements and thought-provoking lyrics. Songs like "A.D.D." showcased their melodic hardcore sound, which featured catchy hooks and intricate guitar work.

Ten Foot Pole's music, while firmly rooted in hardcore, demonstrated the genre's capacity for innovation. Their approach attracted fans who appreciated both the intensity of hardcore and the musical complexity of their compositions. Ten Foot Pole's contribution to the hardcore punk movement highlighted the genre's adaptability and diversity.

### Green Day: From Punk to Pop-Punk

While Green Day is often associated with their later pop-punk sound, their early roots were firmly grounded in the hardcore punk scene of the late 1980s. Formed in 1986 in Berkeley, California, Green Day started as a trio consisting of Billie Joe Armstrong, Mike Dirnt, and drummer John Kiffmeyer (also known as Al Sobrante), later Frank Edwin Wright III (also Known as Tré Cool).

Green Day's early music, exemplified by their 1990 debut album "39/Smooth," reflected the raw and aggressive qualities of hardcore punk. Tracks like "At the Library" and "Going to Pasalacqua" conveyed their youthful energy and a disdain for authority. Although not as prominent in the hardcore punk scene as bands like Sick of It All, Green Day's early contributions showcased the genre's influence.

### DIY Ethos and Political Themes

A defining characteristic of hardcore punk during this era was its unwavering commitment to the DIY ethos. Bands often self-produced records, booked their own shows, and released music through independent labels. This DIY approach was an essential part of the hardcore punk identity, emphasizing self-reliance and resistance to mainstream commodification.

Moreover, hardcore punk frequently addressed political and social issues in its lyrics. Bands used their music as a platform to critique societal norms, advocate for change, and express dissent. The hardcore scene was often associated with progressive and leftist ideologies, reflecting the political consciousness of its participants.

The hardcore punk movement of the late 1980s and early 1990s played a crucial role in revitalizing the broader punk revival. While hardcore remained a distinct subgenre, its influence seeped into other branches of punk music, contributing to a more diverse and dynamic landscape.

The emphasis on DIY ethics and grassroots organizing that characterized hardcore punk continued to influence the punk community as a whole. Independent labels, self-produced records, and a commitment to maintaining authenticity remained central to punk's identity, challenging the homogenizing forces of commercialization.

In conclusion, the late 1980s and early 1990s were marked by the evolution of hardcore punk and its contributions to the broader punk revival. Bands like Sick of It All, Ten Foot Pole, and even Green Day each brought their unique styles and perspectives to the hardcore scene, expanding the boundaries of the genre. This period showcased hardcore punk's adaptability, resilience, and commitment to its DIY ethos and political themes, leaving a lasting impact on the punk music landscape.

# DIVISION.5-5

## Political & Social

The late 1980s and early 1990s were marked by punk's continued engagement with social and political issues. Bands like Anti-Flag, Unwritten Law, and Blink-182 emerged as prominent voices in the punk scene, using their music to address a range of pressing concerns. This section delves into the political dimension of punk during this period, highlighting the bands that carried the banner of social and political activism.

## Anti-Flag: Punks for Progress

Formed in 1988 in Pittsburgh, Pennsylvania, Anti-Flag emerged as a leading force in the punk scene with their unabashedly political lyrics and activism. Their music was characterized by a fast-paced, melodic punk sound, but it was their lyrical content that set them apart. Anti-Flag's songs tackled issues like war, globalization, corporate greed, and social justice.

One of their seminal albums, "Die for the Government," released in 1996, encapsulated their political ethos. Tracks like "You've Got to Die for the Government" and "Police State in the USA" were anthems for those seeking an unapologetic critique of the establishment. Anti-Flag's commitment to political activism extended beyond their music; they were actively involved in various protest movements, advocating for change and social justice.

## Unwritten Law: Social Commentary

Hailing from Poway, California, Unwritten Law gained recognition for their socially conscious lyrics that explored themes like identity, relationships, and the state of society. Their music blended punk rock with alternative and post-grunge elements, creating a distinct sound that resonated with a diverse audience.

Unwritten Law's album "Blue Room," released in 1994, contained songs like "Lame" and "Suzanne" that delved into the complexities of human interaction. Their lyrical depth and willingness to confront challenging issues made them an important voice in the punk scene during this period.

## Blink-182: Injecting Wit and Critique

While Blink-182 is often associated with their playful and irreverent pop-punk sound, their early music contained elements of social critique and political commentary. Formed in 1992 in Poway, California, the band released their debut album "Cheshire Cat" in 1995, featuring tracks like "M+M's" and "Wasting Time."

Blink-182's witty lyrics and sarcastic humour often concealed subtle critiques of societal norms and suburban disillusionment. Their song "Adams' Song," from their 1999 album "Enema of the State," addressed themes of depression and suicide, resonating with many listeners dealing with these issues.

## Punk's Political Engagement

The late 1980s and early 1990s were marked by significant political and social developments. Issues like the Gulf War, environmental concerns, and economic inequality prompted punk bands to engage with the world's challenges. Punk music became a vehicle for critiquing these issues and mobilizing listeners to action.

Punk's political engagement went beyond the stage. Bands like Anti-Flag and Dead Kennedys were actively involved in protests and advocacy work. They saw punk not merely as a form of entertainment but as a means to create awareness and effect change. This activism extended to issues like anti-war protests, environmental conservation, LGBTQ+ rights, and more.

Punk's political activism during this period had a profound impact on the scene and beyond. It not only galvanized the punk community but also influenced the broader youth culture. Punk concerts often doubled as platforms for political awareness, with bands promoting causes and encouraging fans to get involved.

The strong DIY ethos of punk allowed bands to maintain control over their messaging and to avoid commercial co-optation. This self-reliance and commitment to authenticity were integral to the success of punk's political activism.

Punk's influence also extended to the development of social and political movements. Punk music served as a soundtrack for activists and organizers, providing a unifying and empowering force. It inspired a sense of rebellion and a belief in the possibility of change.

In conclusion, the late 1980s and early 1990s witnessed punk's unyielding commitment to social and political activism. Bands like Anti-Flag, Unwritten Law, and Blink-182 used their music as a platform to address pressing issues, from war to mental health. Their lyrics and activism left an indelible mark on the punk scene, inspiring a generation of fans to engage with the world's challenges and pursue meaningful change. Punk, once again, proved itself as a potent voice for those seeking to question authority and create a better world.

# LAST.TRACK.

The punk revival of the 1980s and early 1990s stands as a testament to the enduring power of a subculture born from the streets and fuelled by a rebellious spirit. In this chapter, we embarked on a journey through this transformative era, witnessing how punk not only survived but thrived, evolving in ways that defied expectations and reinvigorated its message.

Throughout this period, punk experienced a remarkable resurgence, expanding its boundaries and resonating with a new generation of fans and musicians. It was a time when punk's ethos of DIY (Do It Yourself) creation and resistance against the status quo remained at its core, even as it branched out into various subgenres and regional scenes.

One of the defining features of this era was the emergence of influential bands that left an indelible mark on punk's history. Bands like Bad Religion, with their thought-provoking lyrics and melodic hardcore sound, demonstrated that punk could be both socially conscious and musically inventive. Suicidal Tendencies fused punk with metal, creating a unique crossover sound that appealed to a wide range of listeners. Meanwhile, The Adolescents captured the vibrant energy of youth culture, channelling it into anthems that spoke to the disenchanted youth of the time.

These bands were part of a broader punk revival that extended across the United States and beyond. The SoCal punk explosion, spearheaded by bands like The Offspring and Pennywise, showcased the diversity and vitality of punk scenes. Punk communities were no longer confined to a few urban centres; they flourished in suburbs, small towns, and even overseas.

The 80s and early 90s were also marked by the rise of politically charged punk music. Dead Kennedys, led by Jello Biafra, used their platform to critique political and social issues, pushing the boundaries of punk's confrontational nature. Songs like "California Über Alles" and "Holiday in Cambodia" remain incisive critiques of the era.

However, this resurgence wasn't without its complexities and controversies. As punk bands like Green Day and Blink-182 achieved mainstream success, questions of authenticity and accusations of "selling out" arose. These debates reflected the tension between punk's countercultural origins and its newfound popularity. While some purists argued that punk should remain underground and uncompromising, others saw these bands as spreading punk's message to a broader audience.

Despite these debates, the 80s and early 90s marked a period of growth and internationalization for punk. Bands from around the world, like Millencolin from Sweden and Refused from Sweden, brought their own unique Flavors to the genre. This global exchange enriched punk music, demonstrating its ability to adapt and incorporate diverse influences while maintaining its core ethos.

As we reflect on this era, it's clear that the legacy of the punk revival continues to shape contemporary music. The bands that emerged during this time, many of which are still active today, serve as a bridge between the original punk movement and the dynamic punk landscape of the 21st century. Their influence can be heard in the work of countless artists who have been inspired by the spirit of rebellion and individualism that defines punk.

In conclusion, the punk revival of the 1980s and early 1990s was a dynamic and multifaceted movement that breathed new life into a subculture many believed had reached its peak in the late 1970s. It was a time of innovation, experimentation, and resilience. Punk music expanded its horizons, appealed to a broader audience, and faced both acclaim and criticism in the process.

Above all, this era reaffirmed the enduring relevance of punk as a cultural force. Punk's ability to evolve, adapt, and remain true to its core values while exploring new territories is a testament to its enduring appeal. It has shown that, even when faced with the contradictions of mainstream success, punk remains a vital and transformative force that continues to inspire rebels, misfits, and music lovers around the world. The story of punk in the 80s and early 90s is a chapter in a larger narrative of punk's resilience and evolution, one that continues to be written to this day.

# DIVISION.6

## Look the Punk

In the world of punk, appearances are far from superficial. They are powerful statements, visual manifestations of rebellion, self-expression, and a steadfast rejection of societal norms. The punk aesthetic is a language in itself, one that boldly proclaims individuality, nonconformity, and the creative spirit of DIY (Do It Yourself) culture. In this chapter, we delve deep into the multifaceted and iconic aspects of punk's visual identity. From the raw creativity of DIY culture to the striking attire and body art that define punk, and the underground infrastructure of independent labels, zines, venues, and festivals that sustains the subculture, we will explore how punk's appearance is not just skin deep but a profound reflection of its ethos.

At the heart of the punk aesthetic is the rebellious spirit of DIY culture. We will embark on a journey through punk's historical roots, tracing the origins of its DIY ethos back to movements and philosophies that reject conventionalism and celebrate individualism. From music production to the creation of zines and grassroots initiatives, we will explore how the punk DIY spirit has been a driving force, empowering individuals to break free from mainstream norms. It is a testament to the transformative power of self-expression, where even the most unconventional ideas find a home.

Punk's visual rebellion finds its most vivid expression in its attire and body art. Leather jackets, torn jeans, band t-shirts, unconventional hairstyles, tattoos, and piercings have become synonymous with punk. In this section, we will trace the evolution of punk fashion from its rebellious origins to its lasting influence on mainstream style. We will explore the role of body art in punk culture and how it extends beyond aesthetics to become a form of protest and identity. Fashion-forward and boundary-breaking, punk attire and body art are not just expressions of style but also powerful tools of dissent.

Shifting our focus to the infrastructure that supports punk culture, we will explore the vital role played by independent record labels, zines, grassroots venues, and punk festivals. These elements are integral in preserving punk's authenticity, fostering a sense of community, and providing platforms for emerging punk artists. Independent labels and zines give voice to underground talent, while grassroots venues and punk festivals offer spaces where punk's rebellious spirit can be experienced firsthand. This section celebrates the diversity and autonomy of the punk ecosystem, showcasing how it thrives beyond mainstream boundaries and contributes to the overall punk aesthetic.

In the pages that follow, we will peel back the layers of punk's visual identity, uncovering the stories, philosophies, and creative energies that have shaped one of the most influential and enduring subcultures in the world. The punk aesthetic is more than just a style; it's a profound reflection of a movement that refuses to conform, challenges the status quo, and empowers individuals to boldly "look the punk."

# DIVISION.6-1

### DIY Culture: Punk's Creative Spirit

The punk aesthetic is a vibrant tapestry woven from threads of rebellion, creativity, and nonconformity. At its core lies the DIY (Do It Yourself) culture, a subversive force that empowers individuals to break free from mainstream norms. This section delves into the historical roots of punk's DIY ethos, tracing it back to movements and philosophies that reject conventionalism and celebrate individualism.

Punk's DIY culture finds its roots in the countercultural movements that rejected established norms, including the Beat Generation of the 1950s and the broader countercultural upheaval of the 1960s. These movements championed personal freedom, self-expression, and the rejection of authority. Figures like Jack Kerouac, Allen Ginsberg, and William S. Burroughs embodied this spirit of dissent and self-reliance in their literary and artistic endeavours. Their rejection of mainstream conventions paved the way for the emergence of the DIY ethos within punk.

One of the most striking manifestations of punk's DIY culture is in music production. Punk artists and bands have often taken matters into their own hands, bypassing traditional music industry gatekeepers. They embraced a philosophy that anyone could form a band, write songs, and perform without the need for formal training or expensive studio sessions. This approach democratized music creation, making it accessible to a wider range of people.

Bands like The Ramones, known for their stripped-down sound and straightforward approach, epitomized the DIY spirit in music. Their music was characterized by short, simple, and high-energy songs that required minimal technical prowess. By demonstrating that musical proficiency was not a barrier to creating impactful music, The Ramones inspired countless aspiring musicians to pick up instruments and start their own bands.

Beyond music, the DIY culture extended into publishing with the rise of punk zines. These homemade, self-published magazines became essential platforms for communication within the punk community. They featured interviews with bands, reviews of records and concerts, political commentary, and personal stories. Zines like "Punk" and "Maximumrocknroll" connected punk scenes around the world and promoted the exchange of ideas.

Grassroots initiatives also flourished under the banner of DIY. Punk communities organized their own concerts, often in unconventional venues such as basements and warehouses, bypassing mainstream music venues. These DIY shows fostered a sense of inclusivity, enabling emerging bands to perform and connect with fans directly. The spirit of collaboration and mutual support was central to the DIY ethos, encouraging individuals to take an active role in their local punk scenes.

DIY culture within punk transcends mere practicality; it is a form of self-expression. Punk fans and artists alike engage in the creation of custom merchandise, from hand-painted band t-shirts to personalized leather jackets adorned with patches and pins. These unique expressions of identity challenge the homogenized ideals perpetuated by mainstream fashion. Moreover, the DIY ethos encourages individualism, asserting that everyone has a voice and can contribute to the punk community. Punk's embrace of self-expression empowers individuals to convey their ideas, frustrations, and passions through music, art, and fashion.

In conclusion, the punk subculture's DIY culture is more than a practical approach to music production and self-publishing. It is a deeply rooted, transformative force that empowers individuals to break free from mainstream norms, celebrate individualism, and express themselves on their terms. This culture has influenced not only the punk movement but also broader notions of creativity, self-expression, and the democratization of culture. In the subsequent sections, we will continue to explore the multifaceted aspects of punk's aesthetic, from its distinctive fashion to its embrace of body art and alternative lifestyles.

# DIVISION.6-2

## Fashion: Punk Attire & Body Art

Punk's visual rebellion is etched into its iconic fashion statements and body art. Leather jackets, torn jeans, band t-shirts, unconventional hairstyles, tattoos, and piercings have become symbols of resistance and individuality. In this section, we embark on a journey through the evolution of punk fashion and explore the role of body art in punk culture. From its rebellious origins to its lasting influence on mainstream style, we uncover how punk attire and body art have not only defined a subculture but also challenged established norms, proving that clothing and body modifications can be forms of protest and identity.

Punk fashion, like the music itself, emerged as a visceral rejection of societal norms. In the early days of punk, often traced back to the 1970s in New York and London, the fashion was characterized by its DIY ethos. Punk musicians and fans repurposed everyday items, transforming them into symbols of rebellion. One of the most iconic punk fashion items was the leather jacket.

These jackets, adorned with patches and pins, served as canvases for self-expression. They defied the polished aesthetics of mainstream fashion and communicated dissent and individuality.

Torn jeans, another hallmark of punk fashion, challenged the idea of clothing as a commodity. Punk rockers would intentionally rip and customize their jeans, turning them into a form of wearable art. This act of destruction and reconstruction was a direct affront to consumerism and conformity. Band t-shirts, often DIY screen-printed, allowed fans to proudly display their musical allegiances. These shirts were not just garments; they were badges of Honor, signifying a connection to a particular subculture and a rejection of mainstream tastes.

Punk's embrace of nonconformity extended to hairstyles. The punk hairstyle became a canvas for creative expression, with brightly coloured mohawks, chaotic spikes, and shaved heads challenging conventional beauty standards. The act of shaving one's head or sporting a bold, unconventional hairstyle was an act of defiance against societal expectations. It was a way of declaring, "I am not like you; I am an individual."

Tattoos and piercings have played a significant role in punk culture, serving as permanent forms of self-expression and resistance. Tattoos became a way for punks to permanently mark their bodies with symbols of rebellion, from political slogans to anarchic imagery. Piercings, particularly in unconventional places like the nose, lip, or eyebrow, challenged the idea of traditional beauty. They were a declaration that one's body belonged to them alone and that societal norms held no sway.

What began as a subculture's visual rebellion eventually seeped into mainstream fashion. The punk aesthetic, with its emphasis on DIY and nonconformity, began to influence haute couture and streetwear alike. Designers and brands began incorporating punk elements into their collections, commodifying the subculture's rebellion. However, this mainstream appropriation often sparked controversy within the punk community, as it seemed to betray the ethos of punk's rejection of consumerism.

Punk attire and body art are not merely fashion choices; they are forms of identity, protest, and expression. They offer individuals a means of challenging established norms, asserting their individuality, and communicating their dissent. For many punks, clothing and body modifications are an integral part of their identity, serving as visual markers of their beliefs and allegiances.

Punk's influence on fashion and body art is enduring. Elements of punk style can still be seen on the streets today, from torn jeans and leather jackets to unconventional hair colours and piercings. The punk ethos of nonconformity and individuality continues to resonate with those who refuse to adhere to mainstream norms.

In conclusion, punk fashion and body art are not superficial adornments but powerful forms of self-expression and resistance. They emerged from a place of dissent, rejecting societal norms and celebrating individualism. Over the years, they have evolved, influenced mainstream fashion, and left an indelible mark on the world of style. Punk has shown that clothing and body modifications can be potent tools for challenging established norms and asserting one's identity and protest. In the following sections, we will delve deeper into the world of punk body art and explore the alternative.

# DIVISION.6-3

### Independent Labels, Zines, Venues, & Festivals

Shifting our focus to the infrastructure that supports punk culture, we explore the vital role played by independent record labels, zines, grassroots venues, and punk festivals. These elements are integral in preserving punk's authenticity, fostering a sense of community, and providing platforms for emerging punk artists. Independent labels and zines give voice to underground talent, while grassroots venues and punk festivals offer spaces where punk's rebellious spirit can be experienced firsthand. This section celebrates the diversity and autonomy of the punk ecosystem, showcasing how it thrives beyond mainstream boundaries and contributes to the overall punk aesthetic.

Independent record labels have been the lifeblood of the punk music scene. These labels, often run by passionate music enthusiasts, provide a platform for punk artists to release their music without compromising their creative integrity. Labels like Epitaph Records, Dischord Records, and Fat Wreck Chords have been instrumental in shaping punk's sonic landscape. They championed bands that embraced the DIY ethos and challenged the conventions of the music industry.

Independent labels not only offer creative freedom but also foster a sense of community. Bands signed to these labels often collaborate and tour together, creating a network of like-minded artists who support one another. The relationship between punk bands and their labels is more than just a business arrangement; it's a partnership built on shared values and a passion for music.

Zines, short for fanzines, are a DIY form of self-published magazines that have been a staple of punk culture since its early days. These homemade publications serve as a platform for punk fans, artists, and writers to share their thoughts, opinions, and artwork. Zines are an essential part of punk's grassroots ethos, allowing anyone with something to say to have a voice.

The content of punk zines is as diverse as the subculture itself. They cover topics ranging from music and politics to personal stories and poetry. Zinesters often use collage art, handwritten text, and photocopied pages, embracing a raw and unfiltered aesthetic that reflects punk's rejection of polished, mainstream media. Zines are a tangible expression of punk's commitment to free speech and the democratization of media.

Grassroots venues are the beating heart of punk culture. These small, independently owned spaces provide a platform for punk bands to perform, connect with their audience, and foster a sense of community. Whether it's a dingy basement club, a converted warehouse, or a DIY punk house, these venues are where the raw energy of punk is unleashed.

Unlike mainstream concert halls, grassroots venues often have minimal rules and regulations. This allows for a greater degree of artistic freedom and experimentation. Punk bands can play loud, fast, and without the constraints of commercial venues. These spaces are where punk's rebellious spirit truly comes to life, where mosh pits form, and where fans and bands blur the line between performer and audience.

Punk festivals are annual gatherings that celebrate the spirit of punk in all its forms. From the renowned Rebellion Festival in Blackpool, UK, to Fest in Gainesville, Florida, these events bring together punk bands, fans, and communities from around the world. Punk festivals are a testament to the global reach and enduring appeal of the subculture.

These festivals are more than just concerts; they are immersive experiences where punk's rebellious ethos is on full display. They often feature a diverse lineup of bands, ranging from punk rock and hardcore to ska and folk punk. Punk festival-goers, often adorned in punk attire and body art, create a vibrant and inclusive atmosphere where individuality is celebrated.

The independent record labels, zines, grassroots venues, and punk festivals collectively form an autonomous ecosystem that thrives beyond mainstream boundaries. They are not driven solely by profit but by a passion for punk and a commitment to its values. This autonomy is what allows punk to retain its authenticity and resist commercialization.

Moreover, this infrastructure plays a crucial role in preserving the diversity of punk culture. It provides a platform for emerging artists and subgenres that may not find a place in the mainstream music industry. It ensures that punk remains a vibrant and ever-evolving subculture, capable of adapting to the changing times while staying true to its core values.

In conclusion, independent record labels, zines, grassroots venues, and punk festivals are the unsung heroes of punk culture. They provide the necessary support and platforms for punk artists and fans to thrive, collaborate, and express themselves freely. They are living proof that punk's rebellious spirit extends far beyond the music itself, shaping every facet of the subculture. In the next chapter, we will explore the global impact of punk, as it transcends borders and resonates with individuals and communities around the world.

# LAST.TRACK.

In this chapter, we have delved deep into the aesthetics of punk, exploring how this subculture has left an indelible mark on the realms of fashion, art, publishing, and independent music. "Look the Punk" has been our guiding principle, and through the lens of punk's creative spirit, we've witnessed a cultural movement that defies convention, embraces the avant-garde, and champions the do-it-yourself ethos.

As we conclude this journey through punk aesthetics, it becomes abundantly clear that punk is far more than just a genre of music—it's a visual and artistic rebellion that refuses to be confined by norms or traditions. Punk's aesthetic legacy is a testament to its unapologetic spirit, a challenge to the status quo, and a celebration of individuality.

Punk's DIY culture has demonstrated that creativity knows no bounds. From fashion to visual arts, punks have shown that innovation thrives when it's free from the constraints of mainstream conventions. The subculture's rejection of consumerism and embrace of self-sufficiency have paved the way for a vibrant world of handmade fashion, provocative art, and independent publishing.

Fashion-forward and boundary-breaking, punk attire and body art have pushed the envelope of self-expression. The ripped clothing, bold hairstyles, and rebellious tattoos are not just symbols of style but statements of defiance. They reflect a rejection of conformity and a commitment to authenticity, reminding us that fashion is not just about aesthetics—it's a declaration of identity.

Independent labels, zines, venues, and festivals have been the lifeblood of punk's creative ecosystem. They have provided platforms for emerging artists, fostered diverse voices, and sustained a thriving subculture outside the mainstream. These DIY spaces have been instrumental in shaping punk's aesthetics, showcasing a spectrum of artistic expressions that challenge, provoke, and inspire.

In the end, punk aesthetics are a testament to the enduring power of counterculture. They are a reminder that creativity and individuality will always find a way to break free from the confines of convention. As we close this chapter, let us carry with us the unyielding spirit of punk's aesthetics—an irrepressible force that dares us to look beyond the ordinary, challenge the norm, and embrace the beauty of the unconventional.

# DIVISION.7

## Global influence

Punk, born in the streets of New York City in the mid-1970s, was initially viewed as a countercultural phenomenon, a spirited rebellion against the excesses of mainstream rock and the suffocating norms of society. However, what began as a local musical movement quickly evolved into a global force of cultural and political significance. Punk's raw energy, DIY ethos, and nonconformist spirit resonated with disaffected youth worldwide, transcending geographic boundaries and language barriers.

Over the years, punk's message evolved to address a wide range of societal and political issues. While the initial wave of punk was characterized by its rejection of mainstream norms and rebellious energy, subsequent generations of punk musicians embraced a more diverse set of concerns. Punk became a platform for addressing issues such as gender equality, LGBTQ+ rights, environmental activism, and more. This evolution showcased punk's ability to adapt and remain relevant in an ever-changing world.

Beyond its music and activism, punk's influence extended to the development of countless subcultures across the globe. From the UK's anarcho-punk scene to Japan's vibrant punk subculture, punk inspired a myriad of interpretations and adaptations. Each new locale brought its unique perspective to the punk ethos, reflecting the distinct challenges and issues faced by local communities.

In this exploration of punk's global influence, we will traverse the continents and delve into the stories, movements, and iconic figures that defined punk in various parts of the world. From the punk rockers of the United States and the anarcho-punks of the United Kingdom to the punk scenes in Latin America, Asia, and beyond, we will uncover the rich tapestry of punk's global legacy. The journey ahead is a testament to the enduring power of punk as a force for change, uniting individuals across borders and inspiring them to make their voices heard.

# DIVISION.7-1

## The Evolution of Punk's Message

Punk, born in the mid-1970s as a raw and rebellious countercultural movement, has undergone a remarkable evolution in its message and concerns over the decades. While its roots are firmly anchored in the rejection of mainstream norms and a confrontational spirit, successive generations of punk musicians have broadened their focus, using their music and activism to address an ever-expanding array of societal and political issues. This transformation has not only showcased punk's adaptability but has also solidified its position as a vital platform for advocating change and social awareness. In this subchapter, we will explore the trajectory of punk's message, from its early days of dissent to its more diverse and inclusive embrace of contemporary concerns.

Punk's origins lie in the economic instability and political disillusionment of the 1970s. Bands like The Ramones, The Sex Pistols, and The Clash served as the vanguard of a sonic revolution, channelling the frustrations and disaffection of disaffected youth into music that openly challenged the status quo. The early punk movement was characterized by its rejection of societal norms and its audacious confrontations with authority figures. Songs like "Anarchy in the U.K." by the Sex Pistols and "White Riot" by The Clash epitomized the rebellious spirit that coursed through punk's veins.

At this stage, punk primarily focused on issues related to alienation, economic disparity, and political discontent. It provided a voice for those who felt marginalized and disenfranchised by mainstream society. Its message was simple and direct, reflecting the urgency and frustration of the times. Punk's ethos revolved around DIY (Do It Yourself) principles, encouraging individuals to take matters into their own hands, create their own music, and challenge the established norms.

As punk continued to evolve, it expanded its thematic scope to encompass an array of pressing societal and political issues. One of the earliest manifestations of this shift was the emergence of anarcho-punk in the late 1970s and early 1980s. Bands like Crass and Discharge infused punk with a strong political agenda, addressing issues such as nuclear disarmament, anarchism, and anti-fascism. Anarcho-punk became a conduit for raising awareness about political activism and dissent.

Simultaneously, punk began to explore themes related to identity and social justice. In the late 1970s, the Rock Against Racism (RAR) movement in the UK used punk as a powerful platform to combat racial tensions and the infiltration of far-right ideologies. Punk bands and fans joined forces to organize concerts and protests that explicitly condemned racism and fascism. This movement brought attention to the issue and united diverse communities under the banner of anti-racism.

Punk's message continued to diversify in the following decades, addressing contemporary concerns that resonated with new generations of punks. As Hunt, E (2019) suggests, in the 1990s, the Riot Grrrl movement emerged, characterized by feminist punk bands like Bikini Kill and Sleater-Kinney. Riot Grrrl tackled issues related to gender equality, sexual harassment, and women's rights. These bands used their music and activism to address deeply ingrained societal norms, challenging the patriarchy both within and outside the punk scene. The Riot Grrrl movement encouraged fans to confront gender-based discrimination and fostered a sense of empowerment through zines, workshops, and protest rallies.

Environmental activism also became a significant theme in punk. Punk bands and fans actively participated in protests against environmental crises and issues such as climate change and deforestation. The punk scene embraced sustainability and eco-consciousness, demonstrating that punk was not just about challenging societal norms but also about advocating for a healthier planet.

In conclusion, punk's message has evolved significantly since its inception. What began as a raw, rebellious rejection of mainstream norms has transformed into a multifaceted platform for addressing a wide range of societal and political concerns. Punk has proven its adaptability, remaining relevant in an ever-changing world by embracing new generations and their unique issues. Whether it's gender equality, LGBTQ+ rights, environmental activism, or other pressing topics, punk has consistently demonstrated its capacity to serve as a powerful catalyst for change and social awareness. As long as there are voices seeking to challenge the status quo, punk will continue to be a resounding and defiant response.

# DIVISION.7-2

## Influence on Subcultures

Beyond its music and activism, punk's influence extended to the development of countless subcultures across the globe. From the UK's anarcho-punk scene to Japan's vibrant punk subculture, punk inspired a myriad of interpretations and adaptations. Each new locale brought its unique perspective to the punk ethos, reflecting the distinct challenges and issues faced by local communities.

Punk, born in the seedy underbelly of New York City in the 1970s, quickly outgrew its humble origins and embarked on a global migration. One of the earliest and most significant stops on punk's world tour was the United Kingdom. In the late 1970s, British youth, disillusioned by the bleak economic landscape and political turmoil, found solace and empowerment in punk's defiant message. Bands like the Sex Pistols and The Clash became the soundtrack of a generation, and the punk movement took root in the UK's social and political landscape. It wasn't just a musical phenomenon; it was a cultural and ideological shift.

The British punk scene quickly splintered into various subgenres, each with its unique characteristics and causes. The anarcho-punk movement, characterized by bands like Crass, Discharge, and Flux of Pink Indians, combined punk's rebellious spirit with a strong emphasis on anarchist ideals. Their music was a rallying cry against the establishment, advocating for DIY ethics, animal rights, and anti-nuclear sentiments. The anarcho-punk scene reflected the prevailing social and political concerns of the era and created a vibrant subculture that would have a lasting impact on the global punk landscape.

## Latin America: Punk as a Vehicle for Social Change

In Latin America, punk emerged as a powerful force for social change during a period marked by political upheaval and social injustice. Bands like Los Violadores in Argentina, Eskorbuto in Spain, and Garotos Podres in Brazil used punk as a platform to address issues such as authoritarian regimes, economic disparities, and human rights abuses. Their music was a rallying cry for those who sought to challenge oppressive governments and bring about societal change.

Punk in Latin America also played a crucial role in fostering a sense of community and resistance. It became a refuge for marginalized youth and a space where they could voice their grievances. Punk's DIY ethos was particularly significant in a region with limited access to resources and venues. Bands often recorded and distributed their music independently, and fans organized underground shows and fanzines to support the scene.

## The Australian Punk Scene

In Australia, punk's influence took root in the 1970s, and it was characterized by a distinctly DIY spirit. Bands like The Saints and Radio Birdman paved the way for a thriving punk scene. Australian punk was characterized by its raw energy and rejection of authority, much like its counterparts around the world. However, it also had a unique flavour that reflected the Australian experience.

The isolation of Australia from the rest of the world played a role in shaping the country's punk scene. Australian bands often had limited access to international punk records and influences, leading to the development of a distinctive sound. The Australian punk scene was closely tied to the local pub culture, with bands frequently performing in small venues and pubs. This grassroots approach gave rise to a tight-knit community of fans and musicians who cherished the DIY ethos and independence of the punk movement.

## Frenzal Rhomb: Aussie Skate Punk Pioneers

Frenzal Rhomb, formed in 1992 in Sydney, exemplifies the vibrant Australian punk scene. The band's fast-paced, melodic, and humorous style, often referred to as "skate punk," resonated with fans not only in Australia but also around the world. Songs like "Never Had So Much Fun" and "Punch in the Face" became anthems of Australian punk, reflecting a blend of catchy melodies and irreverent lyrics.

Frenzal Rhomb's lyrics often tackled social and political issues with a sharp and satirical edge. They were unafraid to voice their opinions on topics such as consumerism, racism, and environmental degradation. The band's outspokenness, combined with their infectious music, endeared them to a wide audience and solidified their place in Australian punk history.

## Bodyjar: Punk Resilience and Adversity

Bodyjar, founded in Melbourne in 1994, brought a different dimension to Australian punk. Their music featured a mix of punk, pop-punk, and skate punk elements, contributing to the diversity of the local punk sound. Albums like "No Touch Red" (1998) and "How It Works" (2000) showcased the band's knack for crafting catchy hooks and anthemic choruses.

The lyrics of Bodyjar often revolved around personal struggles, self-discovery, and resilience in the face of adversity. While they addressed universal themes, their music also reflected the Australian suburban experience, making it relatable to many young Australians. Songs like "Not the Same" and "Hazy Shade of Winter" demonstrated the band's ability to blend introspection with high-energy punk.

## 28 Days: Punk-Rap Fusion

In the late 1990s and early 2000s, 28 Days emerged as a notable force in the Australian punk scene. Hailing from Frankston, Victoria, the band incorporated elements of punk, rap, and alternative rock into their music. Their album "Upstyledown" (2000) featured tracks like "Rip It Up" and "Sucker," which combined punk aggression with rap-infused vocal delivery.

Lyrically, 28 Days addressed themes such as suburban life, youth culture, and personal struggles. Their fusion of punk and rap elements contributed to a distinctive sound that resonated with a diverse audience. While they may not have adhered strictly to punk conventions, their innovative approach reflected the genre's adaptability and willingness to experiment.

The Australian punk scene, characterized by its DIY ethos and unique sound, produced a range of influential bands like Frenzal Rhomb, Bodyjar, and 28 Days. These bands contributed to the global punk landscape by infusing their music with a distinct Australian perspective while addressing both universal and local issues. Their resilience, innovation, and commitment to punk's rebellious spirit continue to inspire new generations of punk enthusiasts, both in Australia and beyond.

### Japan's Punk Subculture: A Fusion of Tradition and Rebellion

In a nation often associated with tradition and conformity, Japan's punk subculture emerged as a striking rebellion against societal norms. Japanese punk bands like The Stalin and GISM fused punk's aggression with a distinctly Japanese flavour. The punk movement in Japan was not just about music; it was an exploration of identity and a challenge to the rigid constraints of Japanese society. It offered a space for Japanese youth to voice their frustrations and aspirations.

Japanese punk bands played a pivotal role in infusing the punk genre with unique elements that resonated with their cultural and social context. Bands like The Stalin, formed in 1980, were known for their confrontational lyrics and aggressive music. Their songs often tackled issues such as political corruption and social inequality in Japan. The Stalin's vocalist, Michiro Endo, delivered his lyrics with a ferocity that mirrored the band's punk ethos.

Another notable Japanese punk band, GISM (God In the Schizophrenic Mind), formed in 1983, pushed the boundaries of punk music even further. They incorporated elements of metal and hardcore punk into their sound, creating a cacophonous and intense sonic experience. GISM's lyrics delved into themes of existentialism, nihilism, and the human condition, challenging traditional Japanese values and philosophies.

Japanese punk was more than just music; it was a cultural and social movement that confronted deeply ingrained norms. In a society where conformity and respect for authority were highly valued, punk represented a radical departure. Japanese youths, often burdened with societal expectations and academic pressures, found solace in punk's rebellious spirit. The subculture provided an outlet for expressing dissatisfaction with the status quo.

Japanese punk bands and their fans actively engaged in protests and demonstrations. They addressed issues such as nuclear disarmament, workers' rights, and environmental conservation. Punk music became a vehicle for raising awareness about pressing social and political concerns in Japan. It was a stark departure from the prevailing image of a nation that adhered to tradition and hierarchy.

What set Japanese punk apart was its fusion of traditional Japanese culture with punk aesthetics. Bands often incorporated elements of traditional Japanese art, clothing, and even musical instruments into their performances. This fusion represented a unique blend of the old and the new, the traditional and the rebellious.

Japanese punk fashion, for instance, often combined punk staples like leather jackets and ripped jeans with traditional Japanese garments like kimonos and hakama. This juxtaposition challenged preconceived notions of what constituted punk attire and reflected a conscious effort to infuse Japanese heritage into the subculture.

Musically, some bands incorporated traditional Japanese instruments, such as taiko drums or shamisen, into their punk compositions. This not only added a layer of complexity to their sound but also served as a symbolic bridge between the punk movement and Japan's rich cultural heritage.

Japanese punk subculture showcased the ability of punk to adapt and incorporate local influences, making it relevant to diverse cultural contexts. It proved that punk was not a one-size-fits-all movement but a dynamic and inclusive force capable of resonating with young people worldwide, regardless of their cultural backgrounds. In Japan, punk became a symbol of resistance against conformity and an assertion of individuality within a society deeply rooted in tradition and societal norms. It demonstrated that punk's rebellious spirit could transcend geographical boundaries and serve as a powerful catalyst for change and self-expression.

## Sweden: Punk Resilience and Melodic Innovation

Sweden, a nation known for its rich musical history, embraced punk with remarkable resilience and an innovative twist. While punk's emergence in Sweden was somewhat delayed compared to the UK and the US, it quickly made up for lost time, leaving an indelible mark on the country's musical landscape. Bands like Refused and Millencolin played pivotal roles in shaping Sweden's punk scene, each offering their unique take on the genre.

### Refused: The Shape of Punk to Come

Refused, hailing from Umeå, Sweden, burst onto the international punk scene in the early 1990s. Their groundbreaking album, "The Shape of Punk to Come" (1998), is widely regarded as a masterpiece that pushed the boundaries of punk rock. With its fusion of hardcore punk, post-hardcore, and avant-garde elements, the album challenged traditional punk conventions. "New Noise," one of the album's standout tracks, became an anthem for punk and post-hardcore enthusiasts around the world.

Lyrically, Refused explored themes of resistance, social change, and the power of collective action. Their songwriting was characterized by intellectual and thought-provoking lyrics that encouraged critical reflection. Refused's influence extended far beyond the punk scene, leaving an indelible mark on various genres and generations of musicians. Their audacious sound and uncompromising message continue to inspire punk and alternative artists worldwide.

### Millencolin: Skate Punk Pioneers

On the other end of the spectrum, Millencolin, formed in Örebro in 1992, is renowned for its energetic and melodic approach to punk. Their skate punk sound, characterized by catchy melodies and harmonious guitar riffs, resonated with a broad audience. Albums like "Pennybridge Pioneers" (2000) catapulted them to international fame. Millencolin's music was not only an auditory delight but also a testament to punk's versatility and ability to embrace diverse subgenres.

Millencolin's lyrics often explored personal experiences, relationships, and the challenges of modern life. Their relatable and heartfelt approach to songwriting struck a chord with fans, transcending language barriers. The band's dedication to touring and performing live further solidified their place in punk history. Millencolin's enduring popularity continues to attract new generations of punk enthusiasts.

### Sweden's Broader Punk Landscape

Beyond Refused and Millencolin, Sweden boasts a rich and diverse punk landscape. The country's punk scene has given rise to numerous bands that have made substantial contributions to the genre. Punk festivals and DIY venues have provided platforms for both established acts and emerging artists to showcase their music.

Sweden's punk influence extends to various subgenres, including crust punk, hardcore punk, and indie punk. Bands like Asta Kask, Moderat Likvidation, and The Hives have left their mark on the Swedish and international punk scenes, each contributing unique elements to the genre. DIY ethics remain a vital part of Sweden's punk culture, allowing independent artists and labels to thrive.

Sweden's punk scene, characterized by its resilience and melodic innovation, has contributed significantly to the global punk landscape. Bands like Refused and Millencolin have showcased the diversity of punk, from its experimental and avant-garde aspects to its catchy and melodic dimensions. Sweden's punk influence continues to inspire artists and fans alike, reaffirming the genre's enduring power to evolve and resonate across borders.

### Punk's Unifying Influence on Subcultures Worldwide

Punk's global influence stretches far beyond the confines of its birthplace, resonating with subcultures around the world. This expansive reach is a testament to its remarkable ability to transcend borders, languages, and cultural barriers. As we reflect on the impact of punk in diverse corners of the globe—from the anarcho-punk scene in the UK to the fusion of tradition and rebellion in Japan, the fight for social change in Latin America, and the DIY spirit in Australia—it becomes evident that punk has served as a unifying force for countless individuals and communities facing unique challenges.

One of the most remarkable aspects of punk's global influence is its capacity to provide a voice for the marginalized and oppressed. In countries like the UK, where anarcho-punk emerged as a powerful subculture, punk became a vehicle for critiquing the prevailing political and economic systems. It allowed disenfranchised youth to channel their discontent into creative and often confrontational expressions. Punk united those who sought to challenge authority and effect change, fostering a sense of solidarity and shared purpose.

In Japan, the fusion of tradition and rebellion within punk gave rise to a unique subculture that grappled with the tension between preserving cultural heritage and pushing the boundaries of societal norms. This hybridized form of punk served as a means of reconciling the past with a desire for cultural evolution. It demonstrated that punk could adapt to local contexts and issues while retaining its core ethos of defiance and self-expression.

In Latin America, punk became a catalyst for social change and a tool for addressing pressing issues such as political oppression and economic inequality. Bands and activists used punk music and aesthetics to challenge authoritarian regimes, advocate for human rights, and create a sense of resistance and resilience. Punk united people in their fight against injustice, showcasing its potential as a unifying and empowering force in the face of adversity.

Australia's punk scene, marked by a strong DIY ethos, reflected a spirit of independence and self-sufficiency that resonated with a country known for its vast landscapes and rugged individualism. Punk communities in Australia emphasized the importance of self-expression, artistic freedom, and inclusivity. They demonstrated that punk's influence could be felt not only in major urban centres but also in more remote regions, reinforcing the idea that punk transcends geography to create a global network of like-minded individuals.

In the end, punk's global influence is a testament to the power of music and culture to foster connections, inspire change, and unite disparate voices. It underscores the idea that punk is more than a genre; it's a philosophy, a mindset, and a vehicle for self-expression and resistance. Across continents and cultures, punk has shown that, when channelled creatively, it has the capacity to empower individuals and communities to address local challenges within a broader global context. Punk is a reminder that, regardless of our backgrounds or circumstances, our shared human experiences can find expression in the unifying language of music and culture.

# LAST.TRACK.

The global journey through punk's influence highlights its remarkable ability to transcend geographical boundaries and resonate with individuals facing diverse challenges. Punk has evolved, adapted, and thrived in various cultural contexts, addressing issues specific to each region while upholding its core values of rebellion, empowerment, and dissent. As punk continues to inspire new generations worldwide, it remains a testament to the enduring power of music and activism to unite people, break barriers, and drive social change. Punk's global legacy is a resounding reminder that, in the face of adversity, voices of dissent will always find a way to be heard.

In conclusion, the global influence of punk has been nothing short of remarkable. What began as a rebellious musical movement in the streets of New York City in the mid-1970s has evolved into a powerful force of cultural and political significance, transcending borders and languages. Punk's message has continuously evolved to address a diverse range of societal and political issues. From its roots in challenging mainstream norms and rebelling against authority, punk has grown to encompass gender equality, LGBTQ+ rights, environmental activism, and more. This evolution exemplifies punk's adaptability and its capacity to remain relevant in an ever-changing world.

Furthermore, punk's impact on subcultures worldwide cannot be understated. It has been instrumental in shaping countless subcultures across the globe, each offering a unique perspective on the punk ethos. From the anarcho-punk scene in the United Kingdom to Japan's fusion of traditional culture with punk aesthetics, punk has inspired diverse interpretations and adaptations. These local expressions reflect the distinct challenges and issues faced by different communities, showcasing punk's ability to resonate on a global scale while maintaining its grassroots authenticity.

Our journey through punk's global impact has taken us across continents, delving into the stories, movements, and iconic figures that have defined punk in various parts of the world. From the punk rockers of the United States and the anarcho-punks of the United Kingdom to the punk scenes in Latin America, Asia, and beyond, we've uncovered the rich tapestry of punk's legacy. This exploration serves as a testament to the enduring power of punk as a force for change, uniting individuals across borders and inspiring them to make their voices heard.

In essence, punk's global resonance is a reminder of its enduring importance in the world. It has served as a symbol of resistance, bringing together people from diverse backgrounds in the pursuit of social and political change. As punk's music and values continue to reverberate through generations, they emphasize the significance of challenging societal norms, amplifying the voices of marginalized communities, and striving for a more equitable and inclusive world. The legacy of punk is not relegated to the past but remains a vital force in the present, inspiring future generations to embrace the punk spirit and uphold its message for years to come.

# DIVISION.8

## Paradox: The Contradiction of Mainstream Punk

Punk, from its inception on the gritty streets of New York City in the mid-1970s, bore the standard of rebellion against the conventions and excesses of mainstream rock and society. It thrived in the underground, where it celebrated raw energy, DIY ethos, and nonconformity. Yet, as punk's influence grew, a curious paradox emerged—punk began to infiltrate mainstream culture. This chapter delves into the intricate dance between punk and the mainstream, exploring the contradictions, ironies, and tensions that arose as punk encountered the very establishment it sought to defy.

Initially, punk was an insurgent force challenging the status quo. However, as time passed, its unmistakable aesthetic, characterized by torn clothing, unconventional hairstyles, and piercing lyrics, started appearing in pop culture. Punk's deliberate rejection of norms and its defiance of authority made it a captivating and subversive element within mainstream media. Its impact on pop culture was paradoxical, both celebrated and critiqued for its disruptive influence on fashion, music, and more.

As punk's allure grew, it collided with the forces of commercialization. Punk's anti-establishment ethos clashed with its rising popularity as a marketable commodity. Punk albums were being produced and sold by major record labels, leading to debates within the punk community. This commercialization paradoxically placed punk at odds with its grassroots, DIY origins. The subculture's purity seemed compromised, creating a dilemma for punk purists and subcultural critics.

The tensions of punk going mainstream escalated as prominent punk bands signed with major record labels, further blurring the lines between the underground and the mainstream. Punk musicians found themselves grappling with paradoxical dilemmas. On one hand, success brought exposure and resources, while on the other, it often threatened the authenticity and ethos of punk music. These tensions came to define the paradoxical relationship between punk and the mainstream.

While punk's infiltration of the mainstream brought about contradictions and challenges, it also led to a transformation of the subculture. Punk's encounters with the mainstream paradoxically influenced its identity, values, and role in society. This chapter delves into how punk managed—or struggled—to reconcile its subversive origins with its newfound prominence, highlighting the ongoing paradox of its existence.

As we navigate the paradoxical terrain of punk's interaction with the mainstream, we will unravel the complexities and consequences of this encounter. This exploration will shed light on the enduring influence of punk's paradoxical journey, both within the subculture and in the broader cultural landscape. It is a testament to the dynamic and ever-evolving nature of punk—a subculture that thrives on contradiction and continues to challenge the status quo.

# DIVISION.8-1

### The Emergence of Punk in Pop Culture

In the mid-1970s, punk rock emerged from the underground music scene of New York City, carrying with it an ethos of rebellion and a rejection of the established norms of mainstream society. Initially, punk was a subculture that thrived on its outsider status, finding its home in dingy clubs and DIY venues. Its unmistakable aesthetic, characterized by torn clothing, unconventional hairstyles, and piercing lyrics, was a deliberate challenge to the polished and manufactured image of mainstream pop culture. Punk's emergence in pop culture marked the beginning of a paradoxical relationship between subversion and mainstream acceptance, a tension that continues to define its legacy.

Punk's roots can be traced back to a time when rock music had become increasingly elaborate and theatrical, with arena rock bands dominating the airwaves. In this environment, punk emerged as a raw, stripped-down response. Bands like The Ramones, The Sex Pistols, and The Clash adopted a do-it-yourself (DIY) ethos, creating music that was intentionally abrasive and anti-establishment. Punk lyrics were confrontational and often laced with political and social critique. These early punk pioneers questioned authority, consumerism, and conformity, setting the stage for a new kind of cultural rebellion.

At its core, punk was a subculture that celebrated outsiders and misfits. Punk fans, often referred to as "punks," rejected the mainstream and embraced a DIY lifestyle. They wore torn clothing adorned with patches and safety pins, and their hairstyles ranged from brightly coloured mohawks to shaved heads. Punk fashion was a deliberate rejection of conventional beauty standards, and it served as a visual representation of punk's defiance. This subversive aesthetic was a direct challenge to the polished and glamorized images promoted by pop culture icons of the time.

As punk bands began to gain notoriety, they infiltrated the mainstream media landscape. Radio stations that had previously played predominantly classic rock and disco started to feature punk songs. This marked the first stage of punk's paradoxical relationship with pop culture. Punk's simplistic and energetic music was a stark departure from the complex and virtuosic rock of the era. Songs like The Ramones' "Blitzkrieg Bop" and The Sex Pistols' "Anarchy in the U.K." became anthems of rebellion that resonated with disaffected youth.

Punk's influence on pop culture extended beyond music. The punk fashion aesthetic, characterized by torn clothing, leather jackets, and bold accessories, began to seep into the mainstream. Mainstream fashion designers incorporated elements of punk style into their collections, resulting in a commercialized version of punk fashion. High fashion brands adapted punk's DIY ethos, transforming it into a luxury trend. The subversive fashion statements of punk were paradoxically commodified, leading to critiques from within the punk community, who saw it as a betrayal of the movement's anti-consumerist roots.

As punk's unmistakable aesthetic and rebellious spirit infiltrated pop culture, a paradox emerged. Punk, which had thrived on its outsider status and rejection of mainstream norms, became a captivating and subversive element within mainstream media. The same subculture that had once sought to tear down the established order was now influencing it. Punk's impact on pop culture was both celebrated and critiqued, with some seeing it as a genuine expression of countercultural ideals and others viewing it as a commercialized and diluted version of the movement.

The emergence of punk in pop culture marked the beginning of a paradoxical journey. Initially a subculture that rejected mainstream norms, punk's unmistakable aesthetic, music, and attitude began to infiltrate and influence pop culture. This interaction was marked by a tension between punk's rebellious ethos and its newfound popularity. In subsequent sections, we will delve deeper into the complexities of punk's relationship with the mainstream, exploring its commercialization and the tensions that arose as it navigated the waters of popular culture. Punk's journey from the underground to the mainstream is a testament to its enduring power as a cultural force that challenges, disrupts, and inspires.

# DIVISION.8-2

## The Commercialization Conundrum

As punk's raw energy and rebellious spirit continued to captivate audiences, it was inevitable that the subculture would collide with the forces of commercialization. Punk, born from the rejection of mainstream norms and corporate control, found itself increasingly intertwined with the very industry it had set out to challenge. This collision of ideals and economic interests led to a paradoxical relationship that placed punk at odds with its grassroots, do-it-yourself (DIY) origins. In this section, we will explore the complexities of punk's commercialization and the tensions it generated within the punk community.

The late 1970s and early 1980s witnessed the rapid rise of punk music and its influence on pop culture. Bands like The Clash, The Sex Pistols, and Ramones had broken through to mainstream audiences, garnering significant attention from major record labels. Punk albums were being produced and distributed on a larger scale, reaching a broader audience than ever before. Punk's raw and uncompromising music, along with its unmistakable fashion, was marketed as a form of rebellion. However, this popularity came at a cost.

At the heart of the commercialization conundrum was the clash of ideals. Punk had emerged as a subculture that celebrated DIY ethics, independence, and a rejection of corporate control. It was a movement that encouraged individuals to pick up instruments, start bands, and create their own music, regardless of technical proficiency. Punk zines, record labels, and underground venues had flourished as part of this independent ecosystem.

The commercialization of punk threatened these ideals. Major record labels saw the potential for profit in punk's rebellious image and marketability, leading to the signing of punk bands to lucrative contracts. This shift from DIY to commercialization raised concerns among punk purists and subcultural critics. It seemed as though punk's purity was being compromised for the sake of profit, leading to a sense of disillusionment within the community.

The "punk sellout" debate became a prominent discourse within the subculture. Some argued that by signing with major record labels and appearing on television, punk bands were betraying their roots and becoming complicit in the corporate machine they had once rallied against. The clash between DIY ethics and commercialization led to accusations of authenticity being compromised. Bands like The Clash, once celebrated for their anti-establishment stance, faced accusations of hypocrisy as they embraced commercial success.

However, it's important to note that not all within the punk community viewed commercialization as inherently negative. Some saw it as a means of reaching a wider audience and spreading the subculture's message of rebellion and nonconformity. The commercialization of punk also brought the subculture's ideals into mainstream discourse, influencing discussions on youth culture and societal norms.

Punk's fashion, which had been a symbol of rebellion and nonconformity, was commodified and sold in shopping malls. Punk-inspired clothing and accessories, often mass-produced and sanitized, found their way into mainstream fashion stores. The same torn jeans and leather jackets that had once been a badge of defiance were now readily available for purchase. This shift raised questions about the authenticity of punk fashion and its transformation into a marketable trend.

Merchandising also became a significant aspect of punk commercialization. Punk bands began to sell branded merchandise, from t-shirts and posters to pins and patches. While this allowed fans to express their allegiance to their Favorite bands, it also contributed to the commercialization of punk culture.

The commercialization of punk represented a paradox within the subculture. On one hand, it brought punk's ideals and aesthetics to a broader audience, challenging societal norms and sparking discussions on rebellion and nonconformity. On the other hand, it raised questions about authenticity, purity, and the clash between DIY ethics and corporate interests. Punk's commercialization conundrum remains a central theme in the subculture's history, highlighting the complex relationship between rebellion and consumerism. In the following sections, we will further explore the tensions that arose as punk navigated its way through the mainstream, shedding light on the paradoxes that continue to define its legacy.

# DIVISION.8-3

### Tensions on the Threshold of Mainstream

The punk subculture emerged as a countercultural force, a spirited rebellion against the conventions of mainstream society. However, as punk's popularity grew, it inevitably collided with the forces of commercialization and the mainstream. This collision resulted in escalating tensions that often-left prominent punk bands at a crossroads. They faced paradoxical dilemmas, where success and exposure clashed with the authenticity and ethos of punk music. In this section, we will delve into the tensions that arose as punk stood on the threshold of the mainstream, defining a complex relationship that has endured over the years.

One of the primary catalysts for the tension between punk and the mainstream was the signing of prominent punk bands by major record labels. As the late 1970s and early 1980s saw the rise of punk music, major labels recognized the potential for profit in this burgeoning subculture. Bands like The Clash, The Sex Pistols, and Ramones were courted by major record labels, offering lucrative contracts and access to a much larger audience.

For these bands, signing with major labels represented an opportunity to reach a broader audience and amplify their messages of rebellion and nonconformity. It provided resources for touring, recording, and promoting their music on a larger scale. However, it also raised concerns within the punk community about the integrity of the subculture and the potential for corporate influence.

The signing of punk bands to major record labels intensified the "punk sellout" debate. The core of this debate revolved around whether punk bands that embraced commercial success were compromising their authenticity and aligning themselves with the corporate machine they had once vehemently opposed. It was a clash of ideals, pitting the DIY ethos of punk against the allure of mainstream recognition.

Bands like The Clash, who had been celebrated for their anti-establishment stance and politically charged lyrics, faced accusations of hypocrisy as they embraced commercial success. Some fans and critics argued that punk's purity was being eroded, leading to a sense of disillusionment within the community. This tension within the punk community was both internal and external, as punk's relationship with the mainstream came under scrutiny from all sides.

The commercialization of punk extended beyond the music itself, influencing the subculture's aesthetics. Punk fashion, characterized by torn clothing, unconventional hairstyles, and DIY sensibilities, began to appear in mainstream fashion. Punk-inspired clothing and accessories, often mass-produced and sanitized, found their way into shopping malls and fashion stores.

What had once been a symbol of rebellion and nonconformity was commodified and sold to the masses. Punk's fashion, which had emerged as a rejection of mainstream norms, was now readily available for purchase in mainstream retail outlets. This transformation of punk fashion into a marketable trend raised questions about the authenticity of punk aesthetics and their evolution in the face of commercialization.

The tensions on the threshold of mainstream underscored a fundamental paradox within punk culture. Success, in the form of major record label deals and mainstream exposure, brought resources and recognition to punk bands. It allowed them to amplify their messages and reach a wider audience. However, this success often raised doubts about the authenticity and purity of punk music.

Punk had been rooted in DIY ethics, independence, and a rejection of corporate control. The collision with the mainstream seemed to compromise these ideals. Nevertheless, some argued that the commercialization of punk culture also brought its ideals into mainstream discourse, challenging societal norms and sparking discussions on rebellion and nonconformity.

The tensions surrounding punk's journey into the mainstream remain a central theme in the subculture's history. The clash of ideals, the "punk sellout" debate, and the impact on punk aesthetics reflect the enduring paradox of punk's relationship with commercialization. Despite the challenges and contradictions brought about by its encounter with the mainstream, punk managed to adapt and transform. Punk subcultures persisted around the world, each with its unique take on the genre. These subcultures continued to challenge norms, foster communities, and use punk's spirit of rebellion to address a wide range of societal and political issues.

# DIVISION.8-4

**Mainstream Evolution: The Rise of Punk Bands**

Punk: a four-letter word loaded with raw energy, nonconformity, and a steadfast commitment to rebellion. Emerging from the underground scenes of New York City and London in the mid-1970s, punk music was a sonic and cultural earthquake that shook the foundations of the music industry. Born out of the frustration and disillusionment of disaffected youth, punk was initially a countercultural movement that thrived on the margins of society. It was loud, abrasive, and unapologetically anti-establishment, providing a voice to those who felt alienated by the excesses of mainstream rock and the stifling norms of a society that seemed out of touch.

Punk's early pioneers, like The Ramones, The Sex Pistols, and The Clash, carved out a rebellious niche, creating a musical and cultural subversion that resonated with legions of fans. But punk's essence was perhaps best captured by its DIY (Do It Yourself) ethos. With this ethos, anyone with a guitar, a message, and a desire to challenge the status quo could be part of the movement. Punk wasn't about virtuoso musicianship; it was about the raw and unfiltered expression of frustration, anger, and disillusionment.

However, as punk grew and its influence spread, a fascinating transformation occurred. Some punk bands, once firmly entrenched in the underground and dedicated to a fiercely independent spirit, found themselves thrust into the spotlight of mainstream music. This chapter delves into the paradoxical journey of punk's evolution, where bands like Green Day, The Offspring, Blink-182, and Sum 41 navigated the treacherous waters between punk authenticity and mainstream stardom.

Our exploration begins with a look back at the early days of punk, the movement's ethos, and the underground scenes that gave birth to these bands. We'll examine how punk's fierce rejection of the mainstream and its commitment to DIY principles laid the foundation for the paradoxical journey that lay ahead.

Next, we'll embark on a journey through the histories and evolutions of each of these bands. From their humble beginnings, marked by small, sweaty punk venues and DIY recordings, to their breakthrough moments that catapulted them into the mainstream spotlight, we'll trace their trajectories with a critical eye on the tensions between punk's rebellious spirit and the allure of commercial recognition.

We'll dissect the pivotal albums and moments that defined their journeys, acknowledging the impact these bands had on both punk and mainstream music. Along the way, we'll explore the critiques and controversies surrounding their transitions, as well as the changing dynamics within the punk subculture.

Finally, we'll reflect on the enduring legacies of these bands and the broader implications of their mainstream success. What did their journeys reveal about the relationship between punk and the mainstream music industry? How did their transformations affect the punk ethos and subculture? And what can we learn from the complex interplay between punk authenticity and mainstream acceptance?

In this chapter, we invite you to join us on a captivating exploration of punk's paradoxical evolution, where the counterculture met the mainstream, and where the spirit of rebellion clashed with the allure of commercial success.

### Green Day – Dookie

Green Day's rise from the gritty confines of the Bay Area punk scene to global superstardom is a tale of both triumph and scrutiny. Their journey, characterized by relentless ambition, musical evolution, and mainstream breakthroughs, underscores the paradox of success within punk culture and the accusations of "selling out."

Green Day, composed of Billie Joe Armstrong (vocals and guitar), Mike Dirnt (bass), and Tré Cool (drums), emerged in the late 1980s in Rodeo, California. They initially performed under the name "Sweet Children" before adopting "Green Day." Influenced by punk pioneers like The Ramones, The Clash, and Operation Ivy, the band honed their craft in the Bay Area's punk clubs. Their early shows were charged with exuberance, memorable melodies, and Armstrong's distinct, raspy voice.

The Bay Area punk scene, known for its history dating back to the late 1970s, provided fertile ground for Green Day's development. Venues such as 924

Gilman Street in Berkeley nurtured budding punk acts, encouraging self-expression and a staunchly DIY ethos. Green Day absorbed these values, which became synonymous with punk culture.

Before their mainstream breakthrough, Green Day released their first two albums, "39/Smooth" (1990) and "Kerplunk" (1992), which laid the foundation for their future success. These records showcased their knack for crafting catchy punk anthems and garnered a dedicated underground following. However, it was their third studio album, "Dookie" (1994), that propelled them to international fame, suggests Green Day Authority (2023).

"Dookie" was a revelation. Produced by Rob Cavallo, the album was brimming with infectious tunes that retained the band's punk roots while infusing a pop sensibility. Tracks like "Basket Case" and "When I Come Around" became instant classics. "Dookie" achieved remarkable commercial success, but this success came with accusations of "selling out" from some quarters of the punk community.

"Dookie" left an indelible mark on the mainstream music industry. At a time when grunge and alternative rock reigned supreme, Green Day's brand of pop-punk injected a surge of energy into the music landscape. The album's success not only revitalized punk but also introduced the genre to a new generation of fans. Green Day's triumph with "Dookie" opened doors for other punk and punk-influenced bands, expanding punk's reach.

However, the mainstream embrace of "Dookie" gave rise to accusations of "selling out." Some die-hard punk purists contended that Green Day had compromised their authenticity and punk ethos in exchange for commercial success. The term "sell-out" within punk culture refers to bands or artists who, in pursuit of fame or fortune, abandon their punk roots, values, or DIY principles. It's a label that carries a certain stigma and has been applied to various bands that transitioned to the mainstream.

In the wake of "Dookie," Green Day faced the challenge of sustaining their momentum and credibility while addressing the "sell-out" allegations. Their subsequent albums demonstrated a commitment to musical evolution and experimentation. "Insomniac" (1995) maintained the raw energy of their earlier work, while "Nimrod" (1997) explored diverse musical territories, including acoustic ballads and ska influences.

In 2000, Green Day released "Warning," a departure from their previous sound, featuring folk and acoustic elements. Though it did not replicate "Dookie's" sales, it showcased the band's versatility. However, it was their 2004 rock opera "American Idiot" that marked a pivotal moment in their career. The album tackled themes of political disillusionment and societal decay, garnering critical acclaim and reaffirming their relevance. While some critics saw this as a response to the "sell-out" accusations, others applauded the band for their artistic growth.

Green Day's journey from the Bay Area punk underground to global stardom exemplifies the dual nature of success within punk culture. "Dookie," their breakthrough album, brought unprecedented fame and commercial triumph but also attracted accusations of "selling out." Yet, Green Day's resilience, evolving sound, and commitment to their craft have allowed them to navigate this paradox successfully. Their legacy remains a testament to the enduring influence of punk, even in the face of mainstream recognition.

### The Offspring - Smash

The Offspring's journey to mainstream recognition, epitomized by their seminal album "Smash" in 1994, is a compelling narrative of punk resilience meeting mainstream triumph. Rooted in the Southern California punk scene, The Offspring's evolution from local punk enthusiasts to international stars illustrates the ongoing debate surrounding the perceived tension between punk authenticity and mainstream success.

The Offspring originated in the sprawling suburbs of Orange County, California, in the early 1980s. Founded by Dexter Holland (vocals and guitar), Greg K. (bass), Noodles (lead guitar), and Ron Welty (drums), the band emerged from the thriving local punk scene. Influenced by bands like Bad Religion, Social Distortion, and Agent Orange, The Offspring's early music was characterized by its raw energy, catchy melodies, and humorous yet often socially aware lyrics.

During the 1980s, The Offspring, like many punk bands, honed their skills through relentless touring, playing small clubs and underground venues across Southern California. They embraced the DIY ethos of punk culture, self-releasing their first albums and self-financing their tours, embodying the authentic spirit of the punk movement.

In 1994, The Offspring released their third studio album, "Smash." Produced by Thom Wilson, who had previously worked with punk legends like Dead Kennedys, the album was a watershed moment for the band. "Smash" retained the band's punk roots but introduced a more polished sound and a heightened sense of melody.

The impact of "Smash" on the mainstream music scene was seismic. The album's energetic and rebellious tracks, including "Self Esteem" and "Come Out and Play (Keep 'Em Separated)," became anthems of a generation. "Smash" eventually achieved multi-platinum status and catapulted The Offspring to international fame. However, this newfound success did not come without its share of scrutiny, with accusations of "selling out" echoing through the punk community.

"Smash" transformed The Offspring from local heroes to global rock stars. The album's fusion of punk aggression with radio-friendly hooks broadened their appeal, attracting a vast and diverse fanbase. While this success brought prosperity and recognition, it also sparked debates about the band's punk authenticity. Some critics within the punk community accused The Offspring of "selling out" by adopting a more accessible sound to achieve mainstream success.

In the wake of "Smash," The Offspring faced the challenge of maintaining their relevance while navigating the "sell-out" allegations. Their subsequent albums, such as "Ixnay on the Hombre" (1997) and "Americana" (1998), continued to showcase their punk sensibilities while exploring diverse musical styles.

The band's ability to transcend the "sell-out" stigma lies in their authenticity and commitment to their punk ethos. They have consistently engaged with social and political issues through their music and maintained a strong connection with their fanbase. Albums like "Conspiracy of One" (2000) and "Splinter" (2003) further solidified their place in the music world.

The Offspring's evolution from the Southern California punk scene to worldwide acclaim with "Smash" exemplifies the complex relationship between punk authenticity and mainstream recognition. Their ability to balance their punk roots with mainstream success and overcome the "sell-out" allegations underscores the enduring influence of punk culture. The Offspring's legacy serves as a reminder that authenticity can persist even in the face of immense popularity.

### Blink-182 - Enema of the State

Blink-182's journey from their raw punk beginnings to their mainstream breakthrough with "Enema of the State" in 1999 epitomizes the concept of "selling out" in punk music. This section delves into the band's formative years, the pivotal release of "Enema of the State," the impact of hit singles like "All the Small Things," and Blink-182's continuous association with the label of "sell-outs" in punk culture.

Blink-182's origin story centres on Poway, California, during the early 1990s when Mark Hoppus (bass/vocals), Tom DeLonge (guitar/vocals), and Scott Raynor (drums) formed the band, initially named "Blink." Infused with the spirit of Southern California's burgeoning punk scene and influenced by bands like Descendents and NOFX, they swiftly gained recognition as a local punk act celebrated for their vigorous live performances and a tongue-in-cheek demeanour.

In their early years, Blink-182 embodied the DIY ethos, taking charge of booking their gigs, independently releasing demos, and hitting the road relentlessly. Their music resonated with a burgeoning generation of punk enthusiasts, leading them to the radar of independent record labels, eventually sealing a deal with Cargo Music.

In 1999, Blink-182 unveiled "Enema of the State," a turning point in their career that would thrust them into the mainstream and catalyse debates about punk "selling out." Produced by Jerry Finn, the album signified a notable deviation from their earlier sound, fusing their punk foundation with a polished production style and pop sensibilities.

"Enema of the State" rapidly achieved multi-platinum status, securing the band's reputation as leaders of the emerging pop-punk wave. The album's path to mainstream prominence initiated a critical dialogue within the punk community regarding whether Blink-182 had forsaken their authentic punk roots for commercial success—a quintessential example of "selling out."

The single "All the Small Things" emerged as the anthem of a generation, propelling Blink-182 into a realm often perceived as the antithesis of punk. Its infectious melody and tongue-in-cheek video lampooning boy bands and pop culture figures propelled the song to chart-topping heights. "All the Small Things" epitomized Blink-182's music—light-hearted yet relatable, rebelling yet accessible.

The cultural sell-out impact of "All the Small Things" extended beyond airwaves. It acted as a conduit bridging the pop-punk subculture and the mainstream, ushering in hordes of new fans. Blink-182's influence on fashion, attitudes, and musical tastes of the late '90s and early 2000s was undeniable, further fanning the flames of the "sell-out" debate.

In the aftermath of "Enema of the State," Blink-182 maintained their relevance by producing albums that showcased their pop-punk proficiency while venturing into various musical territories. Albums such as "Take Off Your Pants and Jacket" (2001) and the self-titled "Blink-182" (2003) demonstrated their maturity as musicians while still retaining their punk essence.

Despite lineup changes and temporary breaks, Blink-182 never strayed far from the "sell-out" label in the eyes of some punk purists. They continued to redefine the boundaries of pop-punk, introducing elements of alternative rock and electronic music into their later works. Their longevity and their capacity to connect with new generations of fans reinforced their status as poster children for the notion of punk "selling out."

Blink-182's trajectory, epitomizing the concept of "selling out" in punk culture, mirrors the broader transformation of pop-punk as a genre. The band's ability to balance punk ethos with mainstream accessibility not only defined their own career but also contributed to the perpetuation of the "sell-out" debate within the genre. Blink-182's legacy stands as a testament to the enduring controversy of punk "selling out" and the intersection of punk authenticity with commercial triumph.

### Sum 41 – All Killer No Filler

Sum 41, a band formed in the late 1990s in Ajax, Ontario, Canada, emerged as a quintessential example of the punk and alternative rock fusion that defined the early 2000s music scene. This section explores the band's origins, their breakthrough album "All Killer No Filler," their mainstream achievements, and their enduring relevance. Additionally, we delve into the accusations of "selling out" that have shadowed their career.

Sum 41 was formed by lead vocalist and guitarist Deryck Whibley, lead guitarist Dave Baksh, bassist and backing vocalist Jason "Cone" McCaslin, and drummer Steve Jocz. Drawing inspiration from punk rock icons like NOFX and Bad Religion, they introduced a unique blend of punk and alternative rock to their music. Sum 41's early work exhibited the raw energy and rebellious spirit associated with punk.

In 2001, Sum 41 unveiled their first studio album, "All Killer No Filler," which stands as a pivotal moment in their career. This record showcased popular tracks such as "Fat Lip" and "In Too Deep." The album's triumph launched Sum 41 into the mainstream, exposing their punk-influenced sound to a worldwide audience.

With the release of "All Killer No Filler," Sum 41 achieved remarkable success. Their catchy melodies, witty lyrics, and high-energy performances resonated with fans worldwide. Songs like "Fat Lip" became anthems of a generation, blending elements of punk, pop, and alternative rock. This mainstream recognition was both a blessing and a curse, as it prompted discussions about whether they had compromised their punk authenticity.

As Sum 41's popularity surged, they faced accusations of "selling out." Some critics argued that their music had become more accessible and radio-friendly, straying from the punk ethos of rebellion and resistance. Additionally, their music videos and appearances in mainstream media sparked debates about whether they had embraced the trappings of commercial success.

Despite the sell-out accusations, Sum 41's musical evolution continued. Subsequent albums like "Does This Look Infected?" and "Chuck" maintained elements of their punk roots while exploring new sonic territories. These releases showcased the band's versatility and growth as musicians. They also demonstrated Sum 41's ability to adapt to changing musical landscapes while staying true to their core identity.

Sum 41's journey from their punk and alternative rock fusion beginnings to mainstream success invites scrutiny of the delicate balance between authenticity and the perception of "selling out." While they navigated through waves of criticism, their impact on the music scene remains undeniable. Sum 41's ability to evolve, experiment, and endure as a band highlights the complexities of maintaining authenticity in the face of commercial success within the punk and alternative rock genres.

### Navigating the Waters of Mainstream Success

In the annals of music history, the journeys of Green Day, The Offspring, Blink-182, and Sum 41 stand as emblematic of the complex and ever-evolving relationship between punk origins and mainstream success. These bands, once firmly rooted in the underground and countercultural realms, embarked on transformative journeys that would take them to the very pinnacles of the music industry.

Green Day, propelled by the iconic "Dookie," crossed the threshold into mainstream acclaim while igniting debates about punk authenticity and "selling out." The Offspring's "Smash" defined an era, showcasing the commercial potential of punk without necessarily compromising its roots. Blink-182's infectious melodies and humour-laden lyrics on "Enema of the State" made them pop-punk icons, attracting both devoted followers and criticism. Sum 41's fusion of punk and alternative rock produced hit songs that resonated globally but also raised questions about the authenticity of their sound.

Each of these bands grappled with accusations of "selling out" as they embraced commercial success. This chapter has examined their evolution, addressing both the compromises made and the authenticity retained. While punk purists may point fingers, it's essential to recognize that navigating the mainstream music industry is a balancing act, one that tests the boundaries of identity and artistic freedom.

As these bands continue to make music and tour worldwide, their legacies persist. They've left an indelible mark on the music industry, demonstrating that, even when faced with the complexities of commercialization, punk roots can remain steadfast. The mainstream may have beckoned, but their influence on contemporary music endures, reminding us that the punk spirit, in all its paradoxes, refuses to be extinguished.

# LAST.TRACK.

Punk, born on the gritty streets of New York City in the mid-1970s, emerged as a subculture and musical movement that revelled in its defiance of mainstream norms. It was a spirited rebellion against the excesses of mainstream rock and the suffocating constraints of society. Rooted in the underground, punk celebrated raw energy, the DIY ethos, and a fierce commitment to nonconformity. However, as punk's influence and allure grew, it embarked on a fascinating and often contradictory journey—the invasion of mainstream culture.

In this chapter, we've delved deep into the intricate dance between punk and the mainstream, unearthing the paradoxes, ironies, and tensions that arose as punk encountered the very establishment it had set out to challenge. We've examined the evolution of punk's message, which expanded to encompass a diverse range of societal and political issues, demonstrating its ability to adapt and remain relevant.

We've explored the global impact of punk, tracing its influence from the United States and the United Kingdom to Latin America, Asia, and beyond, witnessing how local communities infused punk with their unique perspectives and struggles. We've dissected the commercialization conundrum, where punk's anti-establishment ethos clashed with its rising popularity as a marketable commodity. The question of "selling out" reverberated through the narratives of punk bands on their journey to mainstream recognition.

Throughout this chapter, we've travelled alongside bands like Green Day, The Offspring, Blink-182, and Sum 41 as they navigated the complex waters of mainstream success. We've witnessed their evolution, their hits, their sell-out accusations, and their continued relevance in contemporary music.

In the end, the paradox of mainstream punk is a testament to the enduring power of this subculture. Punk's essence, with all its contradictions and complexities, has refused to be diluted by the mainstream. Instead, it has left an indelible mark on the music industry, influencing generations and proving that even as punk broke through the surface, its rebellious spirit remained intact.

As we conclude this chapter, we're left with the understanding that punk, in all its paradoxes, embodies a force of resilience, adaptability, and authenticity. Its journey through the mainstream may have been fraught with challenges, but it stands as a testament to the enduring power of a counterculture that refuses to be tamed. Punk, as paradoxical as it may seem, continues to inspire and provoke, reminding us that rebellion, in all its contradictions, is a force that refuses to be silenced.

# DIVISION.9

## Punk in the Digital Age

Punk, a movement born in the gritty streets of New York City's Lower East Side in the mid-1970s, has always thrived on rebellion and resistance. From its early days, punk music and culture served as a forceful critique of the establishment and a call to arms for disaffected youth. It's a genre that has never shied away from disrupting the status quo, and as we step into the digital age, it's doing just that, but in a whole new way.

Punk's ethos of defiance and DIY (Do It Yourself) has found a natural home in the digital realm. The rise of the internet and digital technology has revolutionized how punk music is created, shared, and experienced. In this chapter, we embark on a journey to explore the dynamic relationship between punk and the digital age.

The first section of this chapter, "Punk's Digital Evolution," delves into how punk has adapted to the digital landscape. Punk's spirit of autonomy and anti-establishment fervour has been mirrored in the way punk bands and communities have harnessed the power of the internet. We'll explore how punk musicians utilize digital tools to create and distribute their music, reaching audiences across the globe without the need for major record labels. The digital era has democratized music production, enabling even the most underground punk bands to have their voices heard.

In the second section, "Social Media and Punk Communities," we'll examine the role of online platforms in shaping contemporary punk culture. Social media platforms like Instagram, Twitter, and TikTok have become vital spaces for punk communities to connect, share music, discuss political activism, and organize events. The internet has allowed punks from different backgrounds and geographic locations to come together, fostering a global network of like-minded individuals. We'll explore how these digital communities have impacted the punk ethos of solidarity and resistance.

The final section, "DIY Recording and Distribution," takes a closer look at how punk musicians have embraced digital recording and distribution methods. The affordability and accessibility of recording equipment and software have enabled punk bands to produce their music independently. Digital platforms like Bandcamp and SoundCloud have become essential tools for punk artists to release their music directly to their fanbase. We'll also examine the challenges and debates surrounding the digital age's impact on the music industry, including issues of piracy, streaming, and artist compensation.

As we navigate the digital rebellion within the punk world, we'll discover how the ethos of punk continues to thrive in the digital age, challenging norms, pushing boundaries, and uniting individuals in the pursuit of authenticity and social change. Punk's journey from the streets to the screens is a testament to its enduring power as a catalyst for rebellion and a symbol of resilience in a rapidly changing world.

# DIVISION.9-1

## Punk's Digital Evolution

The digital age has ushered in a new era for punk, one that aligns remarkably well with the movement's DIY ethos and anti-establishment spirit. While punk was initially a reaction to the excesses of the music industry, it has found a home in the digital landscape where autonomy and grassroots creativity thrive. In this section, we'll delve into the digital evolution of punk, exploring how this countercultural movement has harnessed the power of the internet to create, share, and connect.

At its core, punk has always been about pushing boundaries and challenging norms. In the digital realm, this ethos has taken on new life. Punk musicians, often eschewing the traditional music industry, have embraced digital technology as a means of creating and distributing their music. What was once a movement forged in the backrooms of clubs and basements has now become a global force online.

Punk bands, from established acts to up-and-coming artists, have found the internet to be a powerful tool for music production and dissemination. With affordable recording equipment and software readily available, punk musicians can create their music independently, sidestepping the need for expensive studio time. This shift has allowed for more experimentation and artistic freedom, aligning with punk's tradition of subversion and nonconformity.

One of the most significant changes brought about by punk's digital evolution is the democratization of music production and distribution. The digital age has removed many of the barriers that previously prevented underground punk bands from reaching wider audiences. In the past, signing with a major record label was often seen as the gateway to success. However, the rise of digital platforms has disrupted this traditional model.

Platforms like Bandcamp, SoundCloud, and YouTube have given punk artists the ability to share their music directly with fans, bypassing record labels entirely. This direct-to-audience approach aligns seamlessly with punk's DIY spirit and subversive attitude. Punk musicians can now control every aspect of their music, from recording and mixing to album artwork and marketing, without compromising their creative vision.

The digital age has also fostered a sense of global community among punks. Punk, traditionally a subculture that thrived on local scenes and regional identities, now spans continents and transcends geographic boundaries. The internet has facilitated connections between punk scenes worldwide, creating a vast network of like-minded individuals.

Social media platforms like Instagram, Twitter, and Facebook have become vital spaces for punk communities to interact, share music, and organize events. Punk fans and musicians can now easily connect with peers from different backgrounds and geographic locations, facilitating the exchange of ideas, music, and activism. This global network has not only expanded the reach of punk but has also strengthened its sense of solidarity and resistance.

While the digital age has empowered punk in many ways, it has also brought about its share of challenges and debates. One of the most pressing issues is the proliferation of digital piracy and illegal downloading. Punk's anti-establishment stance often aligns with notions of free music and information, making it susceptible to piracy. This has led to debates within the punk community about the ethics of file sharing and its impact on artists.

Additionally, the rise of music streaming platforms has reshaped the way artists are compensated for their work. While these platforms offer unprecedented access to music, they have also faced criticism for their low royalty rates. Punk, a genre known for its commitment to social and political causes, has been at the forefront of discussions about fair compensation for musicians in the digital age.

Punk's digital evolution represents a renaissance for a movement that has always thrived on rebellion and autonomy. The internet has become a fertile ground for punk musicians and fans alike, enabling them to create, connect, and resist on a global scale. While challenges persist, such as piracy and compensation, the digital age has brought punk back to its DIY roots, empowering artists to control their music and connect with a worldwide community of like-minded individuals. Punk's journey from underground basements to digital platforms is a testament to its enduring spirit of resistance and its ability to adapt and thrive in an ever-changing world.

# DIVISION.9-2

## Social Media & Punk Communities

The digital age has ushered in a profound transformation in the way punk communities connect, communicate, and express themselves. Social media platforms have emerged as vibrant hubs for punk culture, serving as spaces for networking, music sharing, political activism, and the cultivation of a global punk identity. In this section, we'll delve into the multifaceted role of social media in shaping contemporary punk communities, exploring how digital spaces have redefined the very essence of punk culture.

Punk's history is intertwined with a strong tradition of communication through zines, flyers, and underground publications. These analogy methods played a pivotal role in shaping the punk narrative, fostering connections between underground scenes, and disseminating countercultural ideas. In the digital age, social media platforms have become the natural evolution of these DIY communication channels.

Platforms like Instagram, Twitter, and TikTok allow punks to create digital profiles that serve as extensions of their punk identities. Here, they share music recommendations, political messages, art, and personal reflections. Punk communities, once confined to specific geographic regions, have transcended borders. The internet has facilitated a global network of punks who exchange ideas, share experiences, and forge bonds based on shared values of nonconformity and resistance.

One of the most remarkable consequences of social media's integration into punk culture is the globalization of the movement. Punk, which historically thrived on local scenes and regional identities, now spans continents and transcends geographic boundaries. Social media platforms provide punks with unprecedented access to peers from different backgrounds, fostering cross-cultural exchanges and collaborations.

Punk communities on platforms like Instagram have effectively dismantled the geographical constraints that once defined punk scenes. Artists from South America can collaborate with counterparts in Europe, while activists in Asia can learn from the experiences of their North American counterparts. This global network has transformed punk from a localized subculture into a worldwide movement of solidarity, resistance, and collective action.

Social media platforms have also redefined how punk music is created and shared. In the past, punk bands relied on physical recordings, such as vinyl records and cassette tapes, to distribute their music. Today, platforms like SoundCloud and Bandcamp have democratized music production and distribution, allowing even the most underground punk bands to have their voices heard.

SoundCloud, in particular, has become a haven for punk musicians. It provides a user-friendly interface for uploading and sharing music, making it easy for bands to showcase their work to a global audience. Punk musicians can now release songs independently, sidestepping the need for major record labels. This DIY approach aligns seamlessly with punk's tradition of subversion and nonconformity.

TikTok, the short-form video platform, has played a significant role in exposing new audiences to punk music and aesthetics. Through TikTok, punk songs, fashion, and rebellious attitudes have found a home among a diverse and global user base. The platform's algorithm-driven content discovery has helped punk songs go viral, introducing a younger generation to the genre's sounds and ideals.

TikTok challenges traditional notions of punk's exclusivity by making punk accessible to a broader and more diverse audience. It has become a platform for users to share their unique interpretations of punk fashion, music, and identity, pushing the boundaries of what punk can be in the digital age.

Punk has always been a movement with a social and political conscience. In the digital age, this commitment to activism and resistance has found new avenues for expression. Social media platforms are now spaces where punks can organize political actions, share information about protests, and engage in discussions about pressing issues.

For example, the global punk community played a vital role in supporting various social and political movements, such as the Black Lives Matter protests, climate change activism, and LGBTQ+ rights advocacy. Social media allows punks to amplify their voices and create a sense of digital solidarity, mobilizing for causes that align with their punk ethos.

While the digital age has undeniably expanded punk's reach and connected communities worldwide, it has also raised questions about authenticity. The punk ethos has long been associated with independence, nonconformity, and resistance to mainstream norms. In the digital era, where trends can spread rapidly through viral content, some punks have questioned whether the movement's authenticity is compromised.

The internet's power to create overnight sensations has led to debates about what it means to be punk in the digital age. Some argue that the rapid visibility of punk trends on social media platforms dilutes the countercultural spirit, while others see it as a way to introduce punk to new audiences. This debate underscores the complex relationship between punk and the digital landscape.

The digital age has ushered in a punk renaissance, redefining how the movement communicates, creates, and organizes. Social media platforms have become essential tools for connecting global punk communities, sharing music, and advancing political activism. While challenges around authenticity persist, the digital landscape has expanded punk's reach, fostering a sense of global solidarity and collective resistance. Punk's journey from DIY zines to digital profiles represents a continuation of its core values in a rapidly changing world. In this digital age, punk remains a force of autonomy, nonconformity, and rebellion, now on a truly global scale.

# DIVISION.9-3

### DIY Recording & Distribution

In the digital age, punk music has experienced a remarkable transformation in the way it's recorded, distributed, and consumed. The "DIY Recording and Distribution" section of this chapter delves into the evolution of punk's recording processes and how digital tools have empowered punk musicians to create and share their music on their own terms. We'll explore the profound impact of affordability, accessibility, and independence in the realm of punk production and distribution.

Historically, recording music required access to expensive recording studios and professional engineers. For many punk bands, especially those outside major cities, this posed a significant barrier to entry. However, the advent of affordable recording equipment and software has democratized the recording process, allowing punk musicians to capture their sound in bedrooms, garages, and makeshift home studios.

Punk's DIY ethos, which has always celebrated independence and self-sufficiency, aligns seamlessly with this digital recording revolution. Bands like Bad Religion and NOFX have embraced digital recording, producing albums that rival the quality of major studio recordings. The ability to record at home has given punk artists unprecedented creative freedom, enabling them to experiment with their sound without the constraints of studio costs and schedules.

Once punk music is recorded, the next challenge is distribution. Digital platforms like Bandcamp and SoundCloud have emerged as lifelines for independent punk musicians seeking to share their work directly with their audience.

Bandcamp, in particular, has become a staple in the punk community. The platform allows artists to upload their music, set their prices, and connect directly with fans. Punk bands can sell digital downloads, physical merchandise, and vinyl records—all without the need for a traditional record label. This model aligns perfectly with punk's values of autonomy and self-sufficiency.

SoundCloud, on the other hand, offers a space for punk musicians to share their music freely. The platform's user-friendly interface simplifies the process of uploading and sharing tracks, making it accessible for both established bands and newcomers to the punk scene. Punk artists can use SoundCloud to gain exposure, connect with other musicians, and foster a dedicated fanbase.

While the digital age has undoubtedly empowered punk musicians, it has also brought forth a series of challenges and debates. One of the most pressing issues is the proliferation of music piracy. The ease with which music can be shared online has led to concerns about lost revenue and the devaluation of music.

Punk, which has often critiqued the commercialization of music, finds itself in a paradoxical position. The punk ethos of nonconformity and resistance to mainstream norms can clash with the digital landscape, where streaming services dominate and artists are often undercompensated. Some punk musicians and fans grapple with the ethical implications of streaming platforms and seek alternative means of supporting independent artists.

The rise of streaming services like Spotify, Apple Music, and YouTube has transformed how people consume music. While these platforms offer convenience and accessibility, they have also faced scrutiny for their impact on artist compensation. Independent punk bands, in particular, are among those who have questioned the fairness of streaming revenue distribution.

For many punk musicians, streaming services present a conundrum. On one hand, these platforms offer exposure to a global audience, allowing punk music to reach new listeners. On the other hand, the financial returns can be meagre, especially for independent artists with limited streams. This challenge raises questions about the sustainability of punk as a DIY Endeavor in the digital age.

The digital age has ushered in a new frontier for punk musicians, offering unprecedented opportunities for recording, distribution, and connectivity. Punk's commitment to autonomy and nonconformity aligns perfectly with the DIY recording and distribution methods made possible by digital technology. Platforms like Bandcamp and SoundCloud empower punk artists to control their music, reach their audience directly, and maintain their punk ethos.

However, the digital age has also posed challenges, from music piracy to debates about streaming service compensation. These issues prompt discussions within the punk community about how to navigate the complex relationship between punk's values and the digital landscape.

In the end, the digital age has expanded punk's reach and influence, while also raising critical questions about the future of punk music in a rapidly changing music industry. Whether by recording in a bedroom studio or sharing tracks on SoundCloud, punk musicians continue to embody the spirit of DIY resilience, adapting to new technologies while staying true to their rebellious roots.

# LAST.TRACK.

As we conclude this chapter, "Punk in the Digital Age," we reflect on how punk music and culture have not just survived but thrived in the ever-changing digital landscape. The journey through the digital rebellion of punk has been nothing short of transformative. From embracing digital tools for recording and distribution to forming vibrant online communities, punk continues to push the boundaries of what is possible in the digital age.

"Punk's Digital Evolution" showcased how the democratization of music production has allowed punk musicians to capture the essence of their sound independently. The rise of affordable recording equipment and software has liberated punk artists from the confines of traditional recording studios. Bands can now craft their punk anthems in garages, bedrooms, and basements, staying true to the DIY ethos that has always defined the genre.

Digital platforms like Bandcamp and SoundCloud have played a pivotal role in connecting punk bands with their audiences. These platforms empower artists to sell their music directly to fans, eliminating the need for intermediaries like record labels. Punk has demonstrated that independence and creative freedom can coexist within the digital realm.

In "Social Media and Punk Communities," we explored how social media platforms have become essential spaces for punks to connect, share music, and mobilize for change. The internet has facilitated the creation of global networks, allowing punks from diverse backgrounds to unite around shared values of autonomy, resistance, and solidarity.

While punk has a rich history of engaging with political and social issues, social media has amplified its voice. Platforms like Twitter, Instagram, and TikTok have become vehicles for punk activism, providing a platform to challenge societal norms and raise awareness about important causes. The punk ethos of rebellion has found a new home in the digital sphere, where it can challenge authority, question conventions, and inspire collective action.

In "DIY Recording and Distribution," we delved into how digital technology has given punk musicians unprecedented control over their music. The affordability and accessibility of recording equipment and software have allowed punk bands to record their music independently, preserving their unique sound and vision. Platforms like Bandcamp and SoundCloud have empowered artists to release their work directly to fans, bypassing the traditional music industry gatekeepers.

However, this digital revolution has not been without its challenges. Music piracy and debates about streaming service compensation have raised important questions about the sustainability of punk as a DIY Endeavor in the digital age. Punk musicians and fans continue to grapple with the ethical implications of these issues, striving to find solutions that align with their values of autonomy and fairness.

In this digital era, punk remains unplugged and unfiltered. It defies the constraints of mainstream music industry conventions and embraces the power of digital tools to create, connect, and mobilize. The punk spirit of rebellion, autonomy, and nonconformity resonates as strongly today as it did in the basements and garages where the genre was born.

Punk's journey through the digital age has demonstrated its remarkable resilience and adaptability. It continues to challenge norms, question authority, and inspire change, both within the music industry and society at large. As we navigate the digital rebellion, punk reminds us that the essence of the genre lies not in the tools or platforms it employs but in the unyielding commitment to self-expression, resistance, and the pursuit of a better world.

In the digital age, punk remains a beacon of authenticity and a rallying cry for those who dare to defy the status quo. It thrives in the uncharted territory of the internet, reminding us that punk's rebellion is as relevant and essential as ever.

# DIVISION.10

## Punk's Unstoppable Resonance

In the grand tapestry of music and culture, there exists a genre that has always been more than just a genre. Punk, born in the rebellious heart of the 1970s, emerged as a raw, unfiltered expression of discontent, shaking the foundations of both the music industry and society at large. Its influence, far from fading with the passage of time, has only grown stronger, transcending the boundaries of music to seep into art, film, literature, and the very essence of counterculture.

Punk Legacy and Influence invites you to embark on a journey through the lasting impact and enduring resonance of punk. This chapter will dissect the multifaceted legacy that punk has bequeathed to the world, examining its profound influence on music genres, its cultural imprint on art, film, and literature, and the lasting presence of its iconic figures who continue to inspire generations.

Punk music was a defiant response to the excesses and pretensions of mainstream rock in the 1970s. Its loud, fast, and stripped-down sound, often characterized by three-chord structures, challenged the notion that virtuosity was a prerequisite for making meaningful music. But punk's impact didn't stop at its own genre. It was a catalyst for a musical revolution that reverberated across genres and generations.

In this section, we will delve into the myriad ways in which punk has influenced and shaped other music genres. From the alternative and indie rock movements of the 1980s and '90s to the hardcore punk and post-punk subgenres, punk's unapologetic ethos and DIY spirit have left an indelible mark on the music landscape. We'll explore how punk's influence has transcended sound, permeating the very fabric of musical expression.

Punk's influence is not confined to the auditory realm. It has ignited a cultural explosion that has left an indelible mark on art, film, and literature. Punk's disregard for convention and embrace of the avant-garde has inspired artists, filmmakers, and writers to break free from the constraints of tradition and explore new frontiers of creativity.

This section will take you on a journey through the world of punk-infused culture. We'll explore how punk aesthetics have infiltrated the world of visual arts, from the provocative works of Jean-Michel Basquiat to the rebellious photography of Nan Goldin. We'll uncover how punk's confrontational spirit has seared itself onto the celluloid, giving birth to iconic films like "Sid and Nancy" and "Suburbia." And we'll examine how punk's subversive ethos has found its way into the pages of literature, from the visceral prose of William S. Burroughs to the poetic reflections of Patti Smith.

As we move through the annals of punk history, certain names rise above the cacophony, becoming not just musicians but cultural icons. From the snarl of Johnny Rotten to the rebellion of Kathleen Hanna, punk has birthed figures whose influence extends far beyond the stage. These icons have become the embodiments of punk's ethos, the torchbearers of its unyielding spirit.

In this final section, we'll pay tribute to the enduring legacy of punk icons. We'll explore how these figures have continued to shape culture and inspire new generations of rebels and artists. We'll delve into the evolution of punk icons like Iggy Pop and Henry Rollins, tracing their journeys from punk's chaotic beginnings to their enduring impact on contemporary culture. We'll also celebrate the trailblazing women of punk, from Debbie Harry to Poly Styrene, who shattered glass ceilings and redefined punk's gender dynamics.

# DIVISION.10-1

### Influence

As we embark on this exploration of punk's legacy and influence, one thing becomes abundantly clear: punk is not a relic of the past; it is a living, breathing force that refuses to be silenced. Its influence courses through the veins of contemporary music, culture, and counterculture. It challenges us to question authority, embrace individuality, and challenge the status quo.

Punk's resonance is unstoppable, its legacy indomitable. It reminds us that rebellion is not a momentary act but a perpetual state of being, a commitment to authenticity and the unapologetic pursuit of one's truth. Whether you're a seasoned punk aficionado or a curious newcomer, this chapter invites you to immerse yourself in the enduring legacy and untamed influence of punk, a genre that continues to reverberate through time, echoing the call of rebellion in an ever-evolving world.

The annals of music history are punctuated by moments of rebellion and reinvention, and perhaps none have been as audacious and impactful as the emergence of punk. Born from the smouldering ashes of the 1970s, punk music erupted with a ferocity that shattered the complacency of mainstream rock's excesses and pretensions. This seismic shift in musical expression introduced the world to a sound that was loud, fast, and stripped-down, defying the prevailing notion that virtuosity was a prerequisite for making meaningful music. Yet, punk's influence transcended the confines of its own genre, becoming a catalyst for a musical revolution that reverberated across genres and generations.

Before we dive into punk's influence on other music genres, it's crucial to understand the core tenets of punk itself. Punk was more than just a style of music; it was a radical departure from the established norms of the music industry. In the mid-1970s, when punk was birthed on the gritty streets of New York City and the UK, the dominant musical landscape was marked by virtuosic rock acts and indulgent progressive rock bands. Punk's response was a rebellion against this excess, a rejection of technical prowess in Favor of raw, unfiltered emotion.

The sonic characteristics of punk were as defiant as its attitude. Punk songs were often characterized by their brevity, with a "short, sharp shock" approach that delivered powerful messages in under three minutes. Three-chord structures became a defining feature, simplifying music and making it accessible to anyone with a guitar and a desire to express themselves. Bands like The Ramones, The

Sex Pistols, and The Clash exemplified this ethos, crafting anthems that were more about energy, attitude, and authenticity than virtuosic proficiency.

Punk's influence on music genres began to take shape in the aftermath of its initial explosion. In the 1980s, a new wave of bands emerged, drawing inspiration from punk's DIY ethos and rejection of mainstream conventions. These bands would become the pioneers of alternative and indie rock, genres that would dominate the underground and eventually infiltrate the mainstream.

One of the most iconic bands of this era was R.E.M. Hailing from Athens, Georgia, they blended jangling guitars, enigmatic lyrics, and a disdain for rock stardom. R.E.M. demonstrated that you could create meaningful, emotionally charged music without conforming to the stadium rock paradigm. Albums like "Murmur" and "Reckoning" showcased their indie spirit and punk-inspired rejection of the mainstream.

Sonic Youth, another influential band, pushed the boundaries of sound and experimentation. Their dissonant guitar work and avant-garde approach challenged traditional song structures, drawing from punk's ethos of pushing against the boundaries of musical convention. Albums like "Daydream Nation" remain touchstones of alternative rock.

As the 1980s gave way to the '90s, alternative and indie rock continued to evolve. Bands like Nirvana, guided by Kurt Cobain's punk-infused sensibilities, brought grunge to the forefront of the music scene. Their album "Nevermind" was a defining moment, fusing punk's intensity with melodic accessibility and catapulting alternative rock into the mainstream.

While alternative and indie rock were thriving, punk's influence was also percolating in the underground hardcore punk scene. Bands like Black Flag, Minor Threat, and Bad Brains embraced punk's energy but amplified it with breakneck speeds, aggressive riffs, and lyrics that tackled social and political issues head-on.

This hardcore punk movement laid the foundation for a multitude of subgenres, each carrying a piece of punk's DNA. Post-hardcore bands like

Fugazi merged punk's urgency with intricate song structures and emotional depth. Emo, an abbreviation of "emotional hardcore," emerged as a genre characterized by introspective and confessional lyrics, with bands like Sunny Day Real Estate and Jawbreaker blending punk's emotional rawness with melodic sensibilities.

Ska punk, exemplified by bands like Operation Ivy and Rancid, injected punk's rebellious spirit into the infectious rhythms of ska. These bands helped usher in the "third wave" of ska, combining punk's DIY ethos with the danceable grooves of ska's past.

As punk continued to evolve, it gave rise to another genre known as post-punk. Bands like Joy Division, Gang of Four, and The Cure explored new sonic territories, infusing punk's immediacy with experimental and artistic elements. Post-punk retained punk's confrontational spirit but expanded its sonic palette, embracing atmospheric soundscapes, intricate basslines, and poetic lyricism.

Joy Division's "Unknown Pleasures" remains a seminal post-punk album, characterized by its haunting melodies and Ian Curtis's emotionally charged vocals. Similarly, The Cure's "Disintegration" showcased the genre's ability to blend melancholy and innovation.

In the early 1990s, punk's influence reached the Pacific Northwest, where it merged with alternative rock to create the grunge movement. Bands like Nirvana, Pearl Jam, and Soundgarden epitomized grunge's fusion of punk's DIY ethos with a darker, more introspective tone. Grunge's success catapulted alternative rock to the forefront of the mainstream, forever altering the musical landscape.

Nirvana's "Smells Like Teen Spirit" became an anthem for a generation, capturing the disillusionment and disaffection of youth. Kurt Cobain's raw, unpolished vocals and punk-inspired songwriting served as a reminder that music didn't need to be overly complex to be emotionally resonant.

The influence of punk on music genres is a story of rebellion, reinvention, and an unyielding commitment to authenticity. From alternative and indie rock's rejection of mainstream conventions to hardcore punk's aggressive intensity, from the artistic experimentation of post-punk to the emotional catharsis of emo, punk's DNA runs through the veins of contemporary music.

While the sound and style of punk may have evolved and diversified, its spirit remains intact. Punk continues to challenge, provoke, and inspire, a testament to the enduring power of music to defy convention and change the world. As long as there are individuals who dare to question authority, challenge the status quo, and express their unfiltered truths, the influence of punk on music genres will remain an indomitable force, an unapologetic sonic rebellion that refuses to be silenced.

# DIVISION.10-2

## Art, Film, & Literature

Punk's reverberations through the cultural landscape are akin to the aftershocks of a seismic event. Beyond the music, punk has permeated the realms of art, film, and literature, leaving an indelible mark on each. The essence of punk, characterized by its defiance of convention and embrace of the avant-garde, has inspired artists, filmmakers, and writers to break free from the stifling constraints of tradition and explore new frontiers of creativity.

The intersection of punk and visual arts is a crucible of rebellion and raw expression. Punk art refuses to adhere to conventional aesthetics, instead opting for the raw and provocative. One of the most iconic figures in this realm is Jean-Michel Basquiat, whose graffiti-inspired works are a testament to the punk ethos of self-expression. Basquiat's art delves into themes of race, identity, and social inequality, embodying the confrontational spirit of punk.

Nan Goldin, a photographer whose lens captured the raw, unfiltered moments of punk and post-punk life in New York City, took the punk ethos and translated it into visual storytelling. Her intimate photographs document the lives of her friends and lovers, offering a raw and unflinching portrayal of a subculture in flux. Goldin's work, like punk itself, challenges societal norms and celebrates the beauty in imperfection.

Punk aesthetics have also infiltrated the world of graphic design, album covers, and poster art. The iconic imagery associated with punk—ranging from the snarling safety-pin-adorned punk to the DIY collage-style posters for underground shows—has had a lasting impact on visual culture. Punk's irreverent graphic design has become a symbol of rebellion, with its influence seen in everything from street art to fashion.

Punk's influence extends seamlessly into the world of film, where it has birthed a genre that thrives on rebellion, subversion, and gritty realism. One of the most celebrated punk films is "Sid and Nancy," a biographical drama chronicling the tumultuous relationship between Sid Vicious of the Sex Pistols and Nancy Spungen. Directed by Alex Cox, the film captures the nihilistic spirit of punk and explores the darker aspects of fame, addiction, and self-destruction.

"Suburbia," directed by Penelope Spheeris, delves into the lives of disaffected suburban youths who find refuge in a punk house. The film portrays the punk scene's sense of community, rebellion against conformity, and the struggles faced by those on the fringes of society. Its raw and unpolished style mirrors the DIY ethos of punk itself.

Punk has also been a wellspring of documentaries, providing an unfiltered glimpse into the lives of punk bands and their impact. Films like "The Decline of Western Civilization" by Penelope Spheeris and "American Hardcore" by Paul Rachman chronicle the punk scenes of the late '70s and early '80s, offering an oral history of the movement and its enduring legacy.

Punk's influence on literature is a sonic boom of words and ideas that challenge the status quo. Writers have drawn inspiration from punk's confrontational spirit, incorporating its themes of rebellion, alienation, and counterculture into their work.

William S. Burroughs, a literary icon known for his experimental and unconventional writing, intersected with the punk movement. His seminal work, "Naked Lunch," with its fragmented narrative and exploration of addiction and control, resonated deeply with punks who embraced the unconventional. Burroughs's fascination with subversion and resistance mirrored the punk ethos.

Patti Smith, often referred to as the "godmother of punk," has made a profound impact on both music and literature. Her memoir, "Just Kids," provides an intimate glimpse into her relationship with photographer Robert Mapplethorpe and their bohemian life in New York City's punk scene. Smith's poetic prose captures the essence of punk's artistic and personal freedom.

Beyond these notable figures, punk's influence has rippled through contemporary literature. Authors like Irvine Welsh, with his gritty portrayal of Edinburgh's punk subculture in "Trainspotting," have echoed punk's rejection of societal norms and its celebration of the marginalized.

In the realms of art, film, and literature, punk culture has left an indelible mark. It continues to be a wellspring of inspiration for creators who seek to challenge conventions, explore the fringes of society, and celebrate the raw, unfiltered essence of human existence.

Punk's disregard for the conventional paved the way for a new era of creativity that continues to evolve and thrive. Its confrontational spirit, rejection of authority, and celebration of individuality have transcended music, becoming a source of rebellion and inspiration across the cultural spectrum. From the canvas to the celluloid to the printed page, punk's legacy is a testament to the enduring power of counterculture to reshape the artistic landscape.

# DIVISION.10-3

### Legacy of Punk Icons

As we traverse the punk landscape, there emerges a select group of individuals whose names reverberate through time, transcending the boundaries of music to become enduring cultural icons. These figures are more than mere musicians; they are the embodiment of punk's unyielding spirit, the torchbearers of its ethos, and the architects of its legacy.

**Iggy Pop**, often hailed as the "Godfather of Punk," is a force of nature whose influence on the genre cannot be overstated. As the frontman of The Stooges, Iggy personified the chaotic and rebellious spirit of punk before it even had a name. His stage presence, marked by shirtless performances, wild contortions, and self-inflicted injuries, was a precursor to the uninhibited energy that punk would embrace.

Iggy's music was a visceral onslaught of raw power and primal urgency. Tracks like "Search and Destroy" and "I Wanna Be Your Dog" remain punk anthems that continue to ignite frenzied mosh pits and stage dives to this day. Beyond the music, Iggy's audacious persona, with its disdain for convention and authority, set a precedent for punk's confrontational spirit.

**Henry Rollins** is a name synonymous with punk's evolution and the spirit of relentless self-expression. As the frontman for Black Flag, Rollins embodied punk's DIY ethos, touring relentlessly and self-releasing records. His intense stage presence and confrontational performances resonated with audiences seeking an authentic voice in the punk landscape.

Rollins's influence extends far beyond music. He has evolved into a polymath, with careers in spoken word, acting, writing, and activism. His spoken word performances are a testament to his ability to captivate audiences with sharp wit and incisive commentary. Rollins's journey from punk provocateur to a multifaceted artist reflects the transformative power of punk's ethos.

### Women Who Rock

Punk has not been exempt from the broader conversation about gender dynamics, but it has produced trailblazing women who shattered glass ceilings and redefined punk's identity. One such figure is Debbie Harry, the frontwoman of Blondie. Her blend of punk, new wave, and pop created an intoxicating sound that defied categorization. Songs like "Heart of Glass" and "One Way or Another" remain timeless classics.

Poly Styrene, the frontwoman of X-Ray Spex, challenged punk's male-dominated landscape with her fearless presence and socially conscious lyrics. Tracks like "Oh Bondage Up Yours!" were anthems of rebellion and empowerment.

Kathleen Hanna, of Bikini Kill and Le Tigre, used punk as a platform for feminist activism. Her riot grrrl movement addressed issues of gender inequality and sexual violence. Hanna's unapologetic lyrics and powerful stage presence continue to inspire new generations of feminists and punk rockers.

### The Never-Ending Rebellion

The enduring legacy of these punk icons is a testament to the genre's timeless appeal and its power to shape culture. Iggy Pop's wild abandon, Henry Rollins's relentless evolution, and the trailblazing women of punk have left an indelible mark on music, art, and activism. They embody the punk ethos of rebellion, individuality, and self-expression, inspiring new waves of rebels and artists to carry the torch.

As we celebrate the punk icons who have risen above the noise, we recognize that their influence is not confined to a specific era or sound. Their rebellious spirit continues to resonate with those who seek to challenge the status quo, break boundaries, and amplify their voices. Punk is not just a genre; it is a never-ending rebellion, and its icons are the eternal torchbearers of that flame.

# LAST.TRACK.

In the vast, ever-evolving tapestry of music and culture, there exists a genre that defies convention, challenges authority, and transcends time. Born in the tumultuous heart of the 1970s, punk erupted as a raw, unfiltered expression of discontent, a cacophony of voices that shook the foundations of both the music industry and society at large. As we journey through, we find ourselves immersed in the ceaseless echoes of punk's enduring resonance.

Punk, in its essence, has always been more than just a genre; it's a potent force that refuses to be confined. This chapter serves as a compass guiding us through the multifaceted legacy that punk has generously bestowed upon the world. It invites us to explore the profound influence that punk has imprinted upon various facets of our existence, from the diverse realms of music genres to the cultural realms of art, film, literature, and the persistent presence of iconic figures who continue to kindle the fires of rebellion.

Punk's sonic revolution was a defiant response to the excesses and pretensions that had come to define mainstream rock in the 1970s. With its loud, fast, and stripped-down sound, often characterized by rudimentary three-chord structures, punk challenged the notion that virtuosity was a prerequisite for making meaningful music. But punk's revolutionary impact extended far beyond the confines of its own genre. It served as a catalyst for a musical revolution that rippled across genres and generations.

In this section, we delved into the myriad ways in which punk has influenced and transformed other music genres. From the alternative and indie rock movements of the 1980s and '90s to the birth of hardcore punk and post-punk subgenres, punk's unapologetic ethos and DIY spirit have left an indelible mark on the landscape of music. It's a testament to punk's enduring influence that it transcended sound alone, infiltrating the very fabric of musical expression.

Punk's influence doesn't cease at the edge of the stage. It has sparked a cultural explosion, igniting the imaginations of artists, filmmakers, and writers, compelling them to break free from the shackles of tradition and venture into uncharted creative territories.

Our exploration of this section led us through the thrilling world of punk-infused culture. We navigated the visual arts, where punk aesthetics infiltrated the canvas and inspired provocative works by visionaries like Jean-Michel Basquiat. We stepped into the cinematic realm, where punk's confrontational spirit ignited the creation of iconic films such as "Sid and Nancy" and "Suburbia." Finally, we delved into the pages of literature, where punk's subversive ethos found expression in the visceral prose of William S. Burroughs and the poetic reflections of Patti Smith.

As we traversed the annals of punk history, certain names rose above the clamour, transcending the role of mere musicians to become enduring cultural icons. From the snarl of Johnny Rotten to the fierce rebellion of Kathleen

Hanna, punk gave birth to figures whose influence extended far beyond the stage. These icons became living embodiments of punk's ethos, torchbearers of its indomitable spirit.

In this final section, we paid homage to the enduring legacy of punk icons. We delved into their continued influence on culture and their role in inspiring new generations of rebels and artists. We embarked on a journey through the evolutions of punk icons like Iggy Pop and Henry Rollins, tracing their paths from punk's tumultuous birth to their lasting impact on contemporary culture. We also celebrated the trailblazing women of punk, from Debbie Harry to Poly Styrene, who shattered glass ceilings and redefined punk's gender dynamics.

As we conclude our expedition through the legacy and influence of punk, one irrefutable truth emerges: punk is not a relic of the past; it's an unrelenting force that refuses to be silenced. Its resonance courses through the veins of contemporary music, culture, and counterculture. Punk continues to challenge us to question authority, embrace individuality, and challenge the status quo.

Punk's enduring legacy is a testament to its timeless allure and its power to shape culture. Whether you're a seasoned punk aficionado or an intrigued newcomer, this chapter invites you to immerse yourself in the unyielding legacy and boundless influence of punk. It's a genre that continues to reverberate through time, echoing the call of rebellion in an ever-evolving world. Punk is not merely a genre; it's a never-ending rebellion, and its icons are the eternal torchbearers of that flame.

# DIVISION.11

## Controversies & Challenges

Punk, as a genre and a subculture, thrives on the fringes of societal norms, and from its very inception, it's been marked by an uncompromising spirit of defiance. It's a realm where questioning authority is second nature, and challenging conventions is a way of life. Yet, within the anarchic embrace of punk, controversies simmer, and challenges loom large. These controversies aren't signs of punk's decay but rather testaments to its enduring vitality and relevance.

Controversies and Challenges invites you to step into the maelstrom of punk's most contentious debates and formidable obstacles. Here, we'll journey through the heart of the punk community, dissecting the controversies that have torn at its seams and examining the challenges that have tested its authenticity. We'll grapple with the eternal struggle of balancing punk's lofty ideals with the gritty reality of the world it inhabits.

Punk, for all its unity in the face of external opposition, has not been immune to internal strife and ideological battles. In this section, we'll navigate the stormy seas of controversies that have rocked the punk community. From debates over political ideologies and DIY ethics to disputes regarding cultural appropriation and inclusivity, we'll delve into the fierce disagreements that have divided punks.

But in the midst of these controversies, we'll also discover the strength of the punk community—a resilience born from its ability to wrestle with complex issues and emerge with a renewed commitment to its core values. For punk, dissent isn't a weakness; it's a vital sign of life, a reminder that the struggle for authenticity is an ongoing process.

Authenticity has always been the lifeblood of punk, and challenging one's authenticity is the ultimate punk heresy. But in a world where success and commercialization often beckon, staying true to punk's values can become a herculean task. In this section, we'll confront the challenges that have tested punk's authenticity, from accusations of "selling out" to the compromises required to navigate the music industry.

We'll dive into the heated debates over punk bands signing with major labels, the perceived dilution of punk's message for mass appeal, and the tension between punk's DIY ethos and the allure of mainstream recognition. Through these challenges, we'll unearth the age-old question: How does one define authenticity in a world that constantly pushes against its boundaries?

As punk navigates the tumultuous waters of its existence, it grapples with a dilemma that transcends time: How can it uphold its ideals in a world that often resists them? This section delves deep into this enduring struggle, examining how punk confronts the reality of a world that sometimes seems at odds with its values.

We'll explore the paradoxes that have defined punk's journey, from its radical critique of capitalism while operating within a capitalist music industry to its commitment to inclusivity while facing issues of diversity and representation. We'll unravel how punk walks the tightrope between idealism and pragmatism, pushing boundaries while grappling with the constraints of reality.

As we embark on this exploration of punk's controversies and challenges, one thing becomes abundantly clear: punk is a living, breathing entity, constantly evolving and forever challenging. Its controversies and challenges are not signs of weakness but reminders of its unyielding spirit. Punk's battles within and without are reflections of its enduring vitality and relevance in a world that continues to grapple with the very issues punk has been confronting for decades.

This chapter invites you to immerse yourself in the tumultuous world of punk's controversies and confrontations, to grapple with its challenges and dilemmas, and to emerge with a deeper understanding of a subculture that refuses to conform, even to its own expectations. Punk's never-ending battle is a testament to its resilience, and its ongoing relevance serves as a reminder that the fight for authenticity is a struggle worth waging. So, let's dive headfirst into the chaos and cacophony of punk's controversies and challenges, where dissent is a battle cry, and authenticity is a lifelong quest.

# DIVISION.11-1



The punk community, a bastion of countercultural rebellion, may appear to stand united against the world's conformity, but within its ranks, a tempest of controversies has brewed since its inception. It is these internal debates, the clashing of ideals and visions, that have tested the mettle of punk, revealing the depth of its convictions and the scope of its resilience.

Punk's contentious relationship with politics is as old as the genre itself. From the start, it has been a platform for voices demanding social change and criticizing the establishment. However, the diversity of punk's political leanings has led to passionate disagreements. Punk may be synonymous with anarchism for some, but it encompasses a spectrum of beliefs, from left-wing radicalism to right-wing libertarianism.

Debates about punk's political identity have often pitted the idealists against the pragmatists. The fervent activists advocating for a specific agenda sometimes clash with those who view punk as a space for individual expression, not political indoctrination. These debates can be fierce, but they also serve as a testament to punk's capacity to engage in rigorous self-examination.

Punk's essence is intrinsically tied to its DIY (Do It Yourself) ethos. Rooted in the early punk scene, this philosophy encourages self-sufficiency and independence, epitomized by bands producing their music, organizing their gigs, and creating their album covers. However, the evolution of the punk scene has given rise to debates about the integrity of DIY ethics.

As punk gained popularity, some bands signed with major record labels, a move that is often met with accusations of "selling out." Critics argue that by aligning with corporate entities, these bands compromise punk's grassroots authenticity.

This clash between commercial success and DIY principles reveals a deeper tension within punk—a battle between the desire for artistic autonomy and the allure of mainstream recognition.

Punk has always been a melting pot of influences, blending styles and sounds from various cultural backgrounds. However, this eclecticism has occasionally led to debates about cultural appropriation and inclusivity. Some argue that punk's penchant for adopting elements from diverse cultures can be disrespectful and perpetuate stereotypes.

These controversies have sparked discussions about the importance of acknowledging the historical and cultural contexts of punk's influences. They have prompted soul-searching within the punk community, challenging its members to consider whether their pursuit of authenticity should extend to respecting the cultures from which they draw inspiration.

What distinguishes punk from many other subcultures is its capacity to withstand internal discord and emerge stronger. Controversies within the punk community are not signs of weakness but manifestations of punk's vibrant and dynamic nature. Disagreements are not obstacles; they are opportunities for growth.

The punk community's resilience is rooted in its commitment to dialogue and self-reflection. It thrives on debate and dissent, using them as catalysts for evolution rather than as forces of division. It is through these conflicts that punk reaffirms its core values of authenticity, resistance, and independence.

In exploring the controversies within the punk community, we unearth the enduring heart of punk itself. This is not a subculture that seeks comfort in conformity or refuge in uniformity. Punk is a defiant force that thrives on dissent, challenges its own assumptions, and constantly redefines its boundaries.

Controversies within punk are not symptoms of its decline but rather proof of its continued vitality. They are not barriers to unity but stepping stones to deeper understanding. They remind us that punk is not a static entity but a living, breathing, and ever-adapting subculture that remains true to its roots even as it navigates the stormy seas of dissent and discord. Punk's strength lies not in uniformity but in its willingness to confront the complexities of authenticity and rebellion.

# DIVISION.11-2

## Selling Out & Staying True

Punk, by its very nature, is a subculture rooted in rebellion against the establishment and a commitment to authenticity. It thrives on pushing boundaries, challenging norms, and embracing individuality. However, as punk's influence has spread far beyond its underground origins, it has faced significant challenges to its authenticity. This section delves into these challenges, exploring the debates and dilemmas that have arisen.

Perhaps the most potent challenge to punk's authenticity is the accusation of "selling out." For many punk purists, aligning with mainstream institutions, particularly major record labels, is seen as a betrayal of punk's DIY ethos and a compromise of its anti-establishment values. This accusation has been hurled at numerous bands as they transitioned from independent labels to major corporate entities.

The debate over "selling out" is deeply rooted in the tension between punk's desire for artistic freedom and the allure of commercial success. Some argue that signing with major labels provides artists with resources, exposure, and the ability to amplify their message. Others contend that it dilutes the authenticity of punk, rendering it more palatable to mainstream audiences at the expense of its core principles.

As punk bands have gained wider recognition and mainstream success, there is a concern that the message of punk may become diluted or co-opted. Punk's message traditionally emphasizes dissent, rebellion, and a critical examination of societal norms. However, as bands reach larger and more diverse audiences, there is a risk that the core message may be watered down to appeal to a broader demographic.

The tension between retaining punk's confrontational spirit and achieving mass appeal is a significant challenge. Bands may find themselves adapting their image, sound, or lyrics to engage with a wider range of listeners, leading to accusations of compromising their authenticity.

At the heart of punk's authenticity challenge is the clash between its DIY ethos and the lure of mainstream recognition. DIY has always been a core principle of punk, emphasizing self-sufficiency, independence, and creative control. However, the music industry's traditional pathways to success often involve partnering with established record labels, promotional agencies, and corporate entities.

This dilemma has forced many punk artists to navigate a precarious balance. They must decide whether to maintain their DIY principles and limit their reach or embrace the resources offered by the mainstream music industry while potentially sacrificing some of their creative autonomy.

Amid these challenges, the question of what defines authenticity in punk becomes increasingly complex. Does authenticity reside in a band's commitment to its original DIY principles, even if it limits their exposure? Or is authenticity found in a band's ability to adapt and convey its message to a broader audience, even if it means collaborating with mainstream entities?

Punk's history is marked by bands that have faced these dilemmas head-on. Some have chosen to remain firmly rooted in their DIY origins, resisting the temptations of commercialization. Others have embraced mainstream recognition while striving to preserve the essence of punk's authenticity.

The challenges to punk's authenticity reflect the broader tension between rebellion and recognition, authenticity and adaptation. Punk, as a subculture that constantly questions, evolves, and confronts the status quo, remains resilient in the face of these challenges. It reminds us that authenticity is not a static state but a dynamic process, an ongoing struggle to maintain core values while navigating a changing landscape.

Punk's unyielding spirit lies in its ability to engage with these challenges without losing sight of its core principles. Whether through the rejection of corporate influence, the preservation of its confrontational message, or the continued celebration of DIY ethics, punk continues to evolve while retaining its authenticity. It is a testament to the enduring power of rebellion and the unwavering commitment to staying true, even in the face of the most challenging dilemmas.

# DIVISION.11-3

### Balancing Ideals with Reality: The Punk Dilemma

Punk, from its inception, has been a subculture that champions ideals of rebellion, individuality, and authenticity. However, it must grapple with an enduring and complex dilemma: How can it uphold these ideals in a world that often resists and challenges them? This section delves deep into the heart of this struggle, exploring the paradoxes and tensions that have come to define punk's journey.

One of the most striking paradoxes in punk's history is its simultaneous critique of capitalism and its existence within a capitalist music industry. At its core, punk has been a relentless critic of consumerism, corporate greed, and the commodification of art. Yet, punk musicians often operate within a music industry driven by profit and marketability.

Punk bands face the challenge of navigating this paradox. They may reject the trappings of mainstream commercialization while still seeking to reach a wider audience. This dilemma raises questions about the authenticity of punk's anti-establishment stance when it engages with the very institutions it critiques.

Punk has long prided itself on being a subculture that welcomes misfits, rejects, and outsiders. Its commitment to inclusivity is a fundamental part of its ethos. However, the punk scene has also faced criticism for its struggles with diversity and representation.

The challenge of maintaining inclusivity in the face of these critiques forces punk to confront uncomfortable realities. It necessitates addressing issues of sexism, racism, homophobia, and transphobia within the scene. This process can be painful and contentious, as it involves reconciling punk's ideals with the lived experiences of marginalized individuals.

Punk's enduring dilemma revolves around the balance between idealism and pragmatism. On one hand, punk is deeply rooted in idealistic notions of revolution, resistance, and unyielding commitment to values. On the other hand, the real world often imposes limitations, compromises, and complexities that challenge these ideals.

Punk musicians, organizers, and fans constantly navigate this tightrope. They must decide when to embrace idealism, pushing boundaries and challenging norms, and when to embrace pragmatism, recognizing that compromise may be necessary to achieve their goals. This dynamic tension defines punk's struggle to effect meaningful change while acknowledging the constraints of reality.

The punk dilemma, as intricate and paradoxical as it may be, is at the heart of what makes punk an enduring and dynamic subculture. It is not a flaw but a testament to the subculture's capacity for self-examination and evolution.

As punk confronts the challenges of capitalism, inclusivity, and the balance between idealism and pragmatism, it remains a subculture that refuses to succumb to complacency. It embodies the spirit of rebellion against not only external forces but also its internal contradictions.

In its ongoing quest to uphold its ideals in a world that often resists them, punk reinforces the idea that authenticity, inclusivity, and rebellion are not static concepts. Instead, they are ideals worth pursuing, even when the journey is marked by paradoxes and dilemmas. Punk, as a subculture, reminds us that the struggle itself is a testament to the enduring power of its values.

# LAST.TRACK.

In the often chaotic and rebellious world of punk, controversies and challenges have been woven into the very fabric of its existence. As we've journeyed through the tumultuous terrain of "Controversies and Challenges," we've delved into the heart of the punk community, dissecting its internal struggles and external battles. From ideological debates to questions of authenticity and the perpetual dilemma of balancing ideals with reality, punk has faced its fair share of trials. Yet, amidst the discord and dissent, there emerges a story of resilience, evolution, and the enduring spirit of a subculture that refuses to conform.

Firstly, "Controversies Within the Punk Community" revealed that punk, despite its emphasis on unity in the face of external opposition, has been no stranger to internal strife. Debates over political ideologies, DIY ethics, cultural appropriation, and inclusivity have periodically divided punks. However, it's crucial to recognize that these controversies, rather than weakening punk's spirit, have often strengthened its community. Dissent within the punk scene is not a sign of weakness but a manifestation of its commitment to critical thinking and challenging the status quo. Punk has continually evolved by engaging with complex issues and emerging with a renewed sense of purpose.

Secondly, "Challenges to Punk's Authenticity" scrutinized a perennial dilemma that plagues the punk ethos – accusations of "selling out" versus the quest for authenticity in the face of commercialization. Punk's commitment to authenticity is at the core of its identity, and any compromise with mainstream success can be seen as a betrayal of its values. This debate around punk bands signing with major labels and the tension between DIY ethics and mainstream recognition highlights the ongoing struggle to define authenticity within the constraints of the music industry. It prompts us to question what it truly means to remain authentic in a world that often challenges the boundaries of punk's ideals.

Lastly, "Balancing Ideals with Reality" delved into the timeless punk dilemma of upholding its ideals within a world that sometimes resists them. Punk's radical critique of capitalism coexists with its operation within a capitalist music industry. Its commitment to inclusivity faces issues of diversity and representation. These paradoxes embody punk's tightrope walk between idealism and pragmatism, pushing boundaries while grappling with the constraints of reality. This balancing act reflects the subculture's enduring struggle to remain true to its core values while navigating the complexities of an ever-changing world.

In conclusion, the controversies and challenges explored in this chapter are not marks of punk's weakness but symbols of its dynamism and adaptability. Punk's history is a testament to its resilience, as it has weathered internal conflicts and external pressures while preserving its essential character. The subculture's ability to confront these challenges head-on has allowed it to continually evolve and remain relevant, inspiring new generations to question norms, challenge authority, and seek their authentic voices. As we reflect on punk's journey through controversies and challenges, we are reminded that, like the music itself, the punk spirit is loud, defiant, and eternally enduring.

# FINAL.ACT.

## Punk's Future

The final chapter of our journey through the world of punk invites us to peer into the horizon of what lies ahead. As we have explored punk's origins, evolution, controversies, and enduring legacy, we must now turn our gaze to the future. In "Punk's Future," we embark on a speculative journey into the 21st century and beyond, tracing the path that punk has taken since the dawn of a new millennium and examining the emerging trends, challenges, and possibilities that await this indefatigable subculture.

Punk has always been a reflection of the socio-political climate in which it thrives. The turn of the century brought a seismic shift in global events with the tragic attacks on the Twin Towers in New York on September 11, 2001. In the wake of this unprecedented tragedy, punk faced the challenge of responding to a world forever changed by the spectre of terrorism and war.

In this section, we will embark on a journey through the turbulent years following 9/11. We'll explore how punk musicians and communities grappled with the complexities of a post-9/11 world, addressing issues of nationalism, xenophobia, and the erosion of civil liberties. We'll also examine the punk response to the wars in Afghanistan and Iraq and the impact of these events on the subculture's music, lyrics, and activism.

Punk is a genre that thrives on evolution, constantly adapting and reinventing itself. In the 21st century, punk's sonic landscape has continued to evolve, giving rise to new subgenres and sounds that push the boundaries of what punk can be. From the resurgence of garage punk to the fusion of punk with electronic and experimental elements, punk's sonic palette is as diverse as ever.

This section will delve into the emerging trends and sounds that have shaped punk in the new millennium. We'll explore the influence of bands like The Strokes, Arctic Monkeys, and The White Stripes in revitalizing garage and indie punk. We'll also examine the rise of subgenres like folk punk, queercore, and post-punk revival. As punk musicians continue to experiment with sound and style, we'll trace the threads that connect these sonic innovations to punk's rebellious spirit.

The COVID-19 pandemic, a global crisis of unprecedented magnitude, has cast a long shadow over the world. In the face of lockdowns, isolation, and uncertainty, punk communities have faced the challenge of maintaining their resilience, solidarity, and sense of purpose. This section will explore how punk has navigated the tumultuous terrain of the pandemic, reflecting on the ways in which punk musicians and fans have adapted to new modes of creative expression and connection.

We'll examine the role of virtual concerts, livestreams, and online communities in sustaining punk's sense of community and resistance during times of physical distancing. We'll also explore the themes of isolation, anxiety, and social justice that have emerged in punk music and activism in response to the pandemic. As we look to a post-pandemic world, we'll consider how punk's experiences during this global crisis may shape its future trajectory.

Throughout its history, punk has been a force for change, challenging the status quo and advocating for social justice. As we peer into punk's future, we will reflect on its potential to continue driving meaningful change in the world. From climate activism to LGBTQ+ rights, punk has always been a platform for raising awareness and mobilizing communities.

In this final section, we'll explore the role of punk in addressing pressing issues of our time. We'll highlight the activism and advocacy of punk musicians and organizations, from fundraising for charitable causes to promoting political engagement. We'll also examine punk's continued commitment to inclusivity, diversity, and social justice, celebrating the subculture's capacity to inspire positive change.

As we embark on this journey into the future of punk, one thing remains certain: the unwavering spirit of punk endures. It is a spirit that has weathered storms, confronted adversity, and evolved with the ever-changing landscape of culture and society. Punk's future is as boundless as its capacity for rebellion, resilience, and reinvention.

In the chapters that follow, we will explore the post-9/11 era, emerging musical trends, the subculture's response to the pandemic, and its potential to drive future change. It is a journey that invites us to contemplate the enduring significance of punk in a world marked by transformation and uncertainty. Whether you are a lifelong punk enthusiast or a curious newcomer, "Punk's Future" promises to be a provocative exploration of the subculture's evolving role in shaping our world.

# FINAL.ACT.1

## A Brief History of Punk Post 9/11

Punk, with its raw and unfiltered ethos, has always been an uncensored mirror reflecting the social and political landscape of its time. The turn of the 21st century brought forth a seismic shift in global events that would reverberate through every facet of society, and punk was no exception. The tragic and unprecedented attacks on the Twin Towers in New York City on September 11, 2001, marked a turning point that thrust punk into the turbulent currents of a post-9/11 world.

As the dust settled over Lower Manhattan and the world grappled with the shock and horror of the 9/11 attacks, punk communities across the globe found themselves facing a dilemma: How could they respond to a world forever altered by terrorism and the looming spectre of war? The very essence of punk—its irreverence, dissent, and challenge to authority—seemed to demand a response.

In the immediate aftermath of 9/11, punk's response was visceral and unambiguous. The attacks on the World Trade Centre had shaken the world's foundations, and the punk community was quick to voice its outrage and condemnation of the acts of terror. Bands like Anti-Flag, known for their socially and politically charged lyrics, released anti-war anthems that resonated with a generation searching for answers. Songs like "911 for Peace" and "Turncoat" became rallying cries against the impending wars in Afghanistan and Iraq.

The punk scene became a platform for protests and demonstrations, with bands participating in anti-war rallies and benefit concerts. Punk's tradition of political activism and protest music was reignited, as musicians and fans alike raised their voices against militarism, nationalism, and the erosion of civil liberties. Punk's commitment to challenging the status quo found renewed purpose in the face of these global crises.

While punk's response to 9/11 and the subsequent wars was marked by a fervent anti-war stance, it also gave rise to internal debates within the subculture. The paradox of patriotism emerged as some punks grappled with complex emotions of national identity, dissent, and resistance.

Punk, as a subculture founded on rebellion and countercultural values, had often positioned itself in opposition to nationalist fervour. However, the events of 9/11 prompted some punks to reflect on their own sense of identity and belonging. The question of whether it was possible to be both a punk and a patriot sparked passionate discussions within the community.

For some, this internal debate led to a re-evaluation of punk's role in a post-9/11 world. Punk bands and fans began to explore the nuances of dissent and what it meant to be critical of government policies while remaining engaged with the broader issues of national identity and unity. These debates underscored the complexities of navigating punk's principles in a world grappling with fear, grief, and uncertainty.

As punk communities engaged in discussions about patriotism and resistance, the genre's sonic landscape also underwent significant shifts. Punk music has always been adaptable, and the post-9/11 era saw a diverse range of responses in terms of sound and lyrical content.

Some punk bands embraced the genre's tradition of protest music with a renewed sense of urgency. They channelled their anger and frustration into high-energy punk rock anthems that critiqued war, government surveillance, and the erosion of civil liberties. Bands like Rise Against, with songs like "Give It All" and "State of the Union," exemplified this unapologetically political approach.

Conversely, other punk musicians delved into more introspective and sombre territory. The weight of the post-9/11 world prompted a shift towards introspection and self-reflection. Punk bands explored themes of isolation, disillusionment, and the search for meaning in a turbulent world. This introspective strain of punk gave rise to genres like emo and post-hardcore, with bands like Brand New and Taking Back Sunday leading the way.

As we reflect on punk's journey through the post-9/11 landscape, one thing becomes clear: its resilience. Punk's ability to adapt, evolve, and confront complex issues while remaining true to its core values has been a testament to its enduring spirit.

The post-9/11 era presented punk with challenges and dilemmas that demanded introspection and debate. It raised questions about the role of dissent in times of crisis, the complexities of patriotism, and the power of protest music. Yet, punk communities around the world responded with unwavering commitment to their principles, using their music, activism, and solidarity to navigate the turbulent waters of a world forever changed by tragedy.

As we look ahead to punk's future, we carry with us the lessons of resilience, dissent, and the unyielding spirit that has defined this subculture for decades. The post-9/11 era is a chapter in punk's ongoing narrative, a reminder that even in the face of adversity, punk's voice remains as vital and necessary as ever.

# FINAL.ACT.2

## The Evolution of Punk's Sonic Landscape

Punk is a genre defined by its refusal to stand still. Throughout its history, it has embraced change, evolution, and the breaking of musical boundaries. In the 21st century, the punk scene continues to be a fertile ground for innovation, birthing new subgenres and sounds that challenge and expand the genre's sonic landscape. This section explores the emerging trends and sounds that have propelled punk into the future, showcasing the genre's ability to evolve while staying true to its rebellious core.

One of the most notable trends in punk's evolution in the 21st century has been the resurgence of garage punk. This raw and unpolished subgenre draws inspiration from the lo-fi sounds of '60s garage rock and infuses it with punk's trademark energy and attitude. Bands like The Strokes, Arctic Monkeys, and The White Stripes led the charge, breathing new life into garage punk and introducing it to a new generation of music enthusiasts.

The stripped-down, DIY ethos of garage punk aligns perfectly with punk's rebellious spirit. It's characterized by fuzzy guitar riffs, primal drumming, and lyrics that often veer into the realms of love, alienation, and youthful angst. The revival of garage punk served as a reminder that punk's roots lie in simplicity and authenticity, free from the trappings of overproduction.

Folk punk emerged as a significant subgenre in the 21st century, blending the heartfelt storytelling of folk music with punk's irreverence. Bands like Andrew Jackson Jihad (now AJJ), The Front Bottoms, and Days N Daze championed this subgenre, strumming their acoustic guitars while tackling topics ranging from mental health to societal issues.

Folk punk embodies the DIY ethos that has always been at the core of punk. Musicians often self-record and distribute their music, staying true to punk's tradition of independence. The subgenre's lyrical depth and introspective themes have resonated with audiences looking for punk with a different emotional dimension.

Punk has long been a home for outsiders, misfits, and those who challenge societal norms. In the 21st century, the queercore movement emerged, providing a platform for LGBTQ+ artists to express themselves freely within the punk scene. Bands like PWR BTTM and G.L.O.S.S. (Girls Living Outside Society's Shit) pushed boundaries by openly addressing issues of gender identity, sexuality, and inclusivity.

Queercore embodies punk's spirit of rebellion against the status quo, challenging heteronormative and cisnormative ideals. It serves as a powerful reminder that punk is not just a genre but a space where marginalized voices can be amplified and celebrated. Inclusivity has become a central tenet of punk's evolving identity, fostering a more diverse and vibrant community.

The post-punk revival movement rekindled the dark and atmospheric sounds of post-punk bands from the late '70s and '80s. Bands like Interpol, The Killers, and Yeah Yeah Yeahs incorporated elements of punk, new wave, and goth into their music, resulting in a sound that was both haunting and danceable.

This resurgence in post-punk aesthetics showcased punk's ability to reinvent itself while drawing inspiration from its own history. The revival retained the genre's scepticism of authority and convention, often veering into introspective and existential themes. It offered a counterpoint to the more straightforward and aggressive punk subgenres, demonstrating the genre's capacity for complexity.

In the 21st century, punk's sound expanded into new frontiers through experimentation with electronic elements. Bands like Crystal Castles and Death Grips fused punk's rebellious energy with electronic beats and avant-garde production techniques. This fusion created a subgenre known as "digital hardcore" or "experimental punk," pushing the boundaries of what punk could sound like.

The integration of electronic elements challenged the traditional punk sound, but it also demonstrated punk's willingness to embrace innovation. It showed that punk's rebellious ethos could be expressed through a variety of sonic palettes, unafraid to push into uncharted territory.

As we explore the evolving sounds and subgenres within punk, it becomes clear that the genre's capacity for innovation and reinvention is boundless. The 21st century has seen punk remain true to its core values of independence, authenticity, and rebellion while simultaneously expanding its horizons. It continues to be a subculture that thrives on diversity, inclusivity, and the unapologetic pursuit of artistic freedom.

Punk's ability to absorb new influences and challenge conventions has solidified its place in the pantheon of enduring musical genres. Whether through the raw power of garage punk, the introspection of folk punk, the inclusivity of queercore, or the experimentation of electronic-infused punk, the genre remains a dynamic and ever-evolving force that refuses to be confined by the past.

In the face of a rapidly changing world, punk's sonic landscape reflects the subculture's resilience and refusal to conform. As we look toward the future, one thing is certain: punk will continue to evolve, adapt, and inspire, ensuring its place as a vital and enduring force in the world of music and counterculture.

# FINAL.ACT.3

### Punk's Role in the Post-Pandemic World

The COVID-19 pandemic, an unprecedented global crisis, brought the world to a standstill, challenging societies, economies, and cultures alike. Punk, a subculture rooted in resistance and rebellion, faced a unique set of challenges during this period of lockdowns, isolation, and uncertainty. This section delves into how punk communities navigated the uncharted waters of the pandemic, demonstrating resilience, fostering community, and maintaining their spirit of resistance.

With live music venues shuttered and tours cancelled, punk musicians had to find alternative ways to connect with their audiences. Virtual concerts and livestream performances became the norm, allowing bands to reach fans worldwide from the confines of their homes. While nothing could replace the energy of a live punk show, these digital gatherings showcased punk's adaptability and determination to keep the music alive.

Punk communities quickly embraced virtual spaces, organizing and attending online events that brought together fans, musicians, and activists. These events provided a lifeline for an industry that thrives on the live experience. They also demonstrated punk's commitment to its DIY ethos, as bands and fans alike harnessed technology to maintain their connection.

In an era of social distancing, online communities played a pivotal role in sustaining punk's sense of belonging and resistance. Punk forums, social media groups, and digital zines provided platforms for fans to discuss music, share their experiences, and organize virtual events. These digital spaces became lifelines for a community accustomed to the shared camaraderie of punk shows and festivals.

The digital realm also allowed for greater inclusivity within punk communities. People from diverse backgrounds, regardless of geographic location, could participate in discussions, discover new music, and connect with like-minded individuals. The pandemic challenged traditional notions of punk's physical presence and proved that punk's spirit could thrive in the virtual world.

Punk has always been a genre that confronts societal issues head-on, and the pandemic was no exception. Punk musicians responded to the isolation and anxiety brought on by the lockdowns with raw and introspective lyrics. Songs exploring themes of loneliness, mental health struggles, and existential uncertainty resonated with audiences facing similar challenges.

The pandemic also reignited punk's commitment to social justice. As global protests erupted in response to police brutality and systemic racism, punk bands and activists used their platforms to amplify the calls for change. Punk's long history of advocating for marginalized communities found renewed purpose in the fight for racial justice, aligning with movements like Black Lives Matter.

As the world slowly emerges from the shadow of the pandemic, punk faces a future that is both familiar and transformed. The experiences of resilience, community, and resistance during this challenging period have left an indelible mark on the subculture. Virtual events and online communities, once born out of necessity, may continue to play a significant role in punk's landscape, offering new avenues for connection and creativity.

The themes of isolation, anxiety, and social justice that emerged during the pandemic are likely to persist in punk's lyrical and activist expressions. Punk's unapologetic commitment to speaking truth to power remains a potent force for change, and the challenges of the pandemic have only strengthened that resolve.

In a world forever altered by the pandemic, punk serves as a reminder that resistance is not futile; it is necessary. The subculture's ability to adapt, connect, and confront societal issues head-on positions it as a resilient and enduring force in an ever-changing world. The spirit of punk, forged in the crucible of adversity, will continue to inspire generations to come, demonstrating that even in the face of the most daunting challenges, the punk ethos remains unyielding.

# FINAL.ACT.4

### Punk's Potential to Drive Future Change

Punk, born from a spirit of rebellion and resistance, has never been content with merely echoing the status quo. As we peer into the future of punk, we find a subculture poised to continue its legacy of driving meaningful change in the world. From climate activism to LGBTQ+ rights, punk has historically been a platform for raising awareness, mobilizing communities, and pushing for progress.

Punk's commitment to activism has been a constant throughout its history. From the early days of punk, when bands like The Clash tackled issues like unemployment and racial inequality, to the present, punk musicians and communities have consistently used their voices and platforms to advocate for change.

One powerful example of punk activism is the Riot Grrrl movement of the 1990s. Led by bands like Bikini Kill and Sleater-Kinney, Riot Grrrl addressed issues of misogyny, sexual assault, and gender inequality head-on. The movement's fervent DIY ethos empowered women and queer individuals to speak out and create their own spaces within punk.

Punk's political engagement extends beyond the lyrics of its songs. Punk communities have often organized benefit concerts, fundraisers, and charity events to support causes ranging from environmental conservation to homelessness. These initiatives demonstrate punk's dedication to creating positive change in the world.

The 2016 presidential campaign saw a resurgence of political punk activism. Bands like Anti-Flag and Rise Against used their music and influence to encourage young people to vote, participate in protests, and engage in political discourse. Punk's power to mobilize and inspire the next generation of activists remains undiminished.

Punk's ethos of inclusivity and social justice has evolved over the years, reflecting the changing social landscape. The subculture's support for LGBTQ+ rights, racial justice, and gender equality continues to be a driving force for change.

Punk Pride events have become a notable platform for celebrating LGBTQ+ voices within the punk community. Bands like Against Me! and PWR BTTM have broken down barriers and challenged stereotypes, pushing for greater acceptance and representation of queer individuals in punk.

As the climate crisis intensifies, punk's connection to environmental activism grows stronger. Bands and organizations within the punk community are increasingly addressing issues like climate change, deforestation, and animal rights in their music and outreach efforts. Punk has the potential to be a powerful voice in the fight against climate change, using its platform to raise awareness and inspire action.

As we look to the future, punk's potential to drive meaningful change is undeniable. The subculture's history of activism, political engagement, and commitment to social justice positions it as a force for progress in an ever-evolving world. Punk's spirit of resistance remains an enduring source of inspiration, challenging the status quo and demanding a better future.

Punk is not bound by time or place; it thrives on the fringes, in the underground, and in the hearts of those who refuse to accept the world as it is.

It is a reminder that change is possible, that the voices of the marginalized and the oppressed matter, and that the fight for a more just and equitable world is worth every ounce of energy.

In the face of adversity, uncertainty, and the myriad challenges of the future, punk will continue to be a beacon of hope, a catalyst for activism, and a driving force for change. Its potential to inspire generations to come is boundless, reminding us that, in the end, it's not the music alone that defines punk; it's the unyielding commitment to making the world a better place, one loud and rebellious chord at a time.

# FINAL.TRACK.

As we contemplate the future of punk, one thing is abundantly clear: punk is not a genre that rests on its laurels or fades into the background. Rather, it is a subculture defined by its relentless spirit of rebellion and resilience, one that constantly adapts and reinvents itself in response to the ever-changing world.

The new millennium ushered in an era marked by unprecedented global events, none more impactful than the tragic attacks on the Twin Towers in New York City on September 11, 2001. In the aftermath of 9/11, the world underwent profound changes, and punk, as a reflection of the times, was not exempt from these transformations.

Punk's response to the post-9/11 world was marked by a commitment to addressing complex and pressing issues. From critiques of nationalism and xenophobia to protests against the wars in Afghanistan and Iraq, punk musicians and communities confronted the challenges head-on. This period served as a testament to punk's ability to adapt to new socio-political landscapes while staying true to its ethos of dissent.

Punk's resilience is not limited to its socio-political engagement; it also extends to its ever-evolving sonic landscape. The 21st century has witnessed the emergence of new trends and sounds that have expanded the boundaries of what punk can encompass.

Garage punk experienced a resurgence, thanks in part to bands like The Strokes, Arctic Monkeys, and The White Stripes, who revitalized this raw and unpolished subgenre. Folk punk, queercore, and post-punk revival have also made significant strides, showcasing the genre's adaptability to diverse musical influences and identities. This sonic evolution reaffirms punk's status as a subculture that thrives on experimentation and refuses to be confined by conventional boundaries.

The COVID-19 pandemic brought the world to a standstill, presenting an unprecedented challenge to punk communities worldwide. However, punk's resilience shone brightly in the face of adversity.

Punk communities turned to virtual concerts, livestreams, and online forums to maintain their sense of community and resistance during lockdowns. Themes of isolation, anxiety, and social justice emerged in punk music and activism, reflecting the unique challenges of the pandemic era.

As the world navigates a post-pandemic landscape, punk's experiences during this global crisis will undoubtedly shape its future trajectory. The resilience and solidarity demonstrated by punk communities during this time offer hope and inspiration for what lies ahead.

Looking forward, punk's potential to drive meaningful change remains undiminished. Throughout its history, punk has consistently engaged with political and social issues, advocating for progress and justice.

Punk's commitment to activism extends beyond music, with benefit concerts, fundraisers, and charity events being common within the community. Punk musicians have played a pivotal role in encouraging political engagement, particularly among young people, and the subculture continues to be a platform for raising awareness and mobilizing communities. Punk's ethos of inclusivity, diversity, and social justice also continues to evolve, pushing for greater representation and acceptance within the subculture.

In the grand tapestry of music and culture, punk stands as a testament to the enduring power of rebellion, resilience, and authenticity. Its journey from the gritty streets of the 1970s to the complex landscape of the 21st century has been marked by challenges, controversies, and transformations. Yet, through it all, punk has remained a beacon of hope and a catalyst for change.

As we peer into the future of punk, one thing is certain: its spirit is as unyielding as ever. Punk will continue to evolve, adapt, and resist in the face of adversity. It will confront new challenges with the same fervour that has defined it for decades. Whether through sonic innovation, socio-political engagement, or activism, punk's potential to inspire generations to come is boundless.

Punk is not just a genre; it's a philosophy—a commitment to authenticity, a celebration of individuality, and a call to challenge the status quo. Its legacy will continue to reverberate through time, reminding us that, in an ever-evolving world, the voice of dissent and the pursuit of justice are more important than ever. Punk's future may be uncertain, but its resonance is endless, echoing the call of rebellion for generations to come.

# Last.Call.

## A Toast to Punk's Unstoppable Resonance

In the dimly lit back rooms of history, where societal upheaval, artistic rebellion, and audacious dissent converge, a cultural revolution was brewing. It was the late 1970s, a time when music was dominated by disco beats, progressive rock epics, and saccharine pop melodies. But from the gritty streets of New York City to the dingy pubs of London, a seismic shift was occurring, a cultural phenomenon that would come to be known as punk.

Fast forward through the pages of time, and here we stand at the end of our journey through the raucous and rebellious world of punk. In the language of the bar, it's "Last Call"—the final opportunity to raise a glass, share stories, and reflect on the unforgettable experiences that punk has offered us.

Throughout this book, we've navigated the tumultuous waters of punk's history, explored its evolution, dissected its controversies, and celebrated its enduring influence. From the birth of punk on both sides of the Atlantic to its explosive impact on music, fashion, and politics, we've witnessed the audacious spirit of rebellion that refused to be silenced.

We painted a vivid picture of dimly lit clubs where sweat-soaked punks revelled in the raw, unfiltered sound that defined their lives. We donned the torn clothes, the leather jackets, the tattoos, and the defiant attitudes that made up the punk aesthetic—a uniform of non-conformity worn by rebels around the world.

But beyond the fashion, we delved into the heart and soul of punk—the relentless drive for authenticity and resistance against the mainstream. Punk was more than just a genre; it was a call to challenge, disrupt, and transform the world around us. From the DIY ethos that championed self-sufficiency to the confrontational lyrics that tackled issues of injustice and disillusionment, punk proved that music could be a powerful weapon of dissent.

In the world of punk, we met iconic figures who embodied the spirit of rebellion. From the snarl of Johnny Rotten to the fiery determination of Kathleen Hanna, these punk icons became torchbearers of an unyielding ethos. They broke boundaries, shattered glass ceilings, and inspired new generations of rebels and artists.

But as we reflect on this journey, we must acknowledge that "Last Call" doesn't mean the end of punk—it's an invitation to celebrate its unstoppable resonance. Punk, born in the rebellious heart of the late 1970s, has proven time and again that it cannot be confined to the annals of history. Its influence courses through the veins of contemporary music, culture, and counterculture.

Punk challenges us to question authority, embrace individuality, and challenge the status quo. It reminds us that rebellion is not a momentary act but a perpetual state of being, a commitment to authenticity and the unapologetic pursuit of one's truth. Whether you're a seasoned punk aficionado or a curious newcomer, "Last Call" invites you to immerse yourself in the enduring legacy and untamed influence of punk, a genre that continues to reverberate through time, echoing the call of rebellion in an ever-evolving world.

So, as we raise our glasses in this final toast, let us remember the dimly lit back rooms of history, where punk was born—a cultural revolution that defied convention, embraced authenticity, and refused to be silenced. Here's to the rebels, the misfits, and the iconoclasts who continue to shape our world through the unstoppable force of punk.

# BIBLIOGRAPHY.


Brenner, B. (2016). *Joey Ramone Fought the OCD Stigma and More.* http://theocddiaries.com/uncategorized/joey-ramone-fought-the-ocd-stigma-and-more/

Gilmore, M. (2016). *The Curse of The Ramones.* https://au.rollingstone.com/music/music-news/the-curse-of-the-ramones-1189/

Green Day Authority. (2023). Green Day Biography: Part 2. https://www.greendayauthority.com/band/biography.php?part=2

History.com Editors. (2021). *The Ramones play their first public gig at CBGB in downtown Manhattan.* https://www.history.com/this-day-in-history/the-ramones-play-their-first-public-gig-at-cbgbs-in-downtown-manhattan

Hunt, E. (2019). *A brief history of Riot Grrrl – the space-reclaiming 90s punk movement.* https://www.nme.com/blogs/nme-blogs/brief-history-riot-grrrl-space-reclaiming-90s-punk-movement-2542166

Likewolf. (2023). The Punk Rock Attitude. https://likewolf.com/punk-rock-history

MasterClass. (2021). Hardcore Punk Music Guide: History and Bands of Hardcore. https://www.masterclass.com/articles/hardcore-punk-music-guide

McCabe, S. (2020). *The 500 Greatest Albums of All Time.* https://www.rollingstone.com/music/music-lists/best-albums-of-all-time-1062063/

Palumbo, M. (2018). *The Beat Generation.* https://20thcenturyhistorysongbook.com/song-book/the-fifties/the-beat-generation/

West, J. (2015). *Lost, beat, blank: the punk unconscious in subversive and trangressive cultural productions.* https://scholarworks.utrgv.edu/cgi/viewcontent.cgi?article=1184&context=leg_etd

Whiteley, S. (2013). Women and Popular Music: Sexuality, Identity, and Subjectivity. Routledge.

Wyatt, C. (2023). The Clash and Their Musical Influences. https://www.punktuationmag.com/the-clash-and-their-musical-influences/

# Appendix

AMERICAN HARDCORE. (2023). http://www.americanhardcorebook.com/

Andersen, M., & Jenkins, M. (2003). Dance of Days: Two Decades of Punk in the Nation's Capital.

Bessman, J. (1993). Ramones: An American Band.

Cogan, B. (2010). The Encyclopedia of Punk.

Fast 'n' Bulbous. (2023). http://www.fastnbulbous.com/

Gimarc, G. (2005). Punk Diary: The Ultimate Trainspotter's Guide to Underground Rock.

Henry, T. (1989). Break All Rules! Punk Rock and the Making of a Style.

Heylin, C. (2007). Babylon's Burning: From Punk to Grunge.

Laing, D. (2015). One Chord Wonders: Power and Meaning in Punk Rock.

Maximum Rocknroll. (2023). http://www.maximumrocknroll.com/

McNeil, L., & McCain, G. (2016). Please Kill Me: The Uncensored Oral History of Punk.

Moore, R. (2009). Sells Like Teen Spirit: Music, Youth Culture, and Social Crisis.

No Echo. (2023). http://www.noecho.net/

Ogg, A. (2007). No More Heroes: A Complete History of UK Punk from 1976 to 1980.

O'Hara, C. (2000). The Philosophy of Punk: More than Noise!

Raha, M. (2004). Cinderella's Big Score: Women of the Punk and Indie Underground.

Reddington, H. (2007). The Lost Women of Rock Music: Female Musicians of the Punk Era.

Reynolds, S. (2006). Rip It Up and Start Again: Postpunk 1978-1984.

Robb, J., & Rollins, H. (2012). Punk Rock: An Oral History.

Rombes, N. (2009). A Cultural Dictionary of Punk: 1974-1982.

Sabin, R. (1999). Punk Rock: So What? The Cultural Legacy of Punk.

Salewicz, C. (2008). Redemption Song: The Ballad of Joe Strummer.

Savage, J. (1992). England's Dreaming: Anarchy, Sex Pistols, Punk Rock, and Beyond.

Spitz, M., & Mullen, B. (2001). We Got the Neutron Bomb: The Untold Story of LA Punk.

Strongman, P. (2008). Pretty Vacant: A History of UK Punk.

Thompson, S. (2004). Punk Productions: Unfinished Business.

www.ingramcontent.com/pod-product-compliance
Lightning Source LLC
Chambersburg PA
CBHW051320130726
47987CB00004B/1879